D!RTY®

CHINESE

Everyday Slang from "What's Up?" to "F*%# Off!"

MATT COLEMAN
EDMUND BACKHOUSE

illustrated by **LINDSAY MACK**

D0004221

Ulysses Press

Published by:
Ulysses Press
P.O. Box 3440
Berkeley, CA 94703
www.ulyssespress.com

ISBN: 978-1-56975-727-7
Library of Congress Control Number: 2009902019

Printed in Canada by Webcom

10 9 8 7 6 5

Acquisitions Editor: Nick Denton-Brown
Managing Editor: Claire Chun
Editor: Jon Babcock
Copyeditor: Lauren Harrison
Interior Design: what!design @ whatweb.com
Cover Design: Double R Design
Production: Abigail Reser
Back Cover Illustration: Lindsay Mack

Distributed by Publishers Group West

For Paul, an 89-year-old Chinese-American gentleman I met in a bar yesterday who has an even fouler mouth than I do!

TABLE OF CONTENTS

·····Acknowledgments

Matt: Thanks to Brendan O'Kane, who taught me how to say, "fuck [my] grandpa's piss-stinking asshole," Hans Cui, the Canto-Canuck for his infinite filthiness, Huang Sui for her long distance kinkiness, Shanghai Lane for the long Logo sessions, Catherine Mathes and Derek Sandhaus for teaching me "how to get my swerve on," Nick, Keith, and the good people at Ulysses Press for their endless patience, last but not least the Godfather of the China Blog Mafia—John Pasden—for hooking this up, keeping it real, and for teaching us all the dirty words we know in English and Chinese (We won't tell about the kittens, John!).

Edmund: For my parents, who taught me better, and my teachers, who will hopefully read this with the good humor and tolerance that got them through their classes with me. Thanks to Song Li for her patience, and Ulysses Press, for theirs.

USING THIS BOOK

Dirty Chinese assumes you know enough Chinese to get around, and if you don't—that is, unless you really think it's a good idea to learn how to say "fistfucking" before you can order food—then you might want to put this down, put a few months into getting a grounding, and come back later. It's cool, we'll still be here.

The dirty little secret about "Chinese" is that it doesn't exist: it's a family of languages, rather than a single language, and a speaker of Cantonese will be able to understand a speaker of Mandarin about as well as a Portuguese person can understand a speaker of Italian. When we say "Chinese" throughout this book, we're really referring to Modern Standard Mandarin, or putonghua—the national language of the People's Republic of China. Some of the terms here may be more Beijing-y (these are mostly from Edmund) or more Shanghai-y (these are mostly from Matt), but all of them should be generally understood anywhere proper Mandarin is spoken. In some cases we've added Taiwanese slang terms, but in general we've confined ourselves to Mainland Mandarin so that in a few years when Taiwan gets "liberated" into the ground, this book will still be current.

All of the sentences in this book are given in English, then in the Hanyu Pinyin Romanization, then in characters. (We've gone with simplified characters throughout the book.) There's a quick and dirty guide to Hanyu Pinyin below, and you may want to take some additional time to get yourself up to speed with the system before reading on, just to make sure that every come-on, every blistering insult, every slurred request for "Jus' onnnnne more" hits home.

•••••(Quick and) dirty Chinese (pronunciation)

We know, we know—you want to get straight to the dirty bits, and we'll be happy to take you there in a second. But there's nothing worse than telling someone that you'll kick their ass so hard their ancestors will feel it eight generations back only to find that they couldn't understand what you were saying, so here's a quick guide to making yourself basically understandable.

•••••The tones

The first tone is high, level, and held a little longer than the other tones. The second tone starts around the middle of your range and rises quickly to the top. The third tone starts around the middle, drops very quickly to the bottom of your range, then rises sharply to the top. The fourth tone starts at the top of your range and drops quickly to the bottom. Tones also sometimes change depending on what tones they're surrounded by; the details of this are head-explody, but the most common example—where two third tones become a second tone and a third tone (so that 你好 nǐhǎo is actually pronounced níhǎo) is easy enough to remember.

•••••Pinyin

Hanyu Pinyin is the standard way of writing Chinese using the Roman alphabet. There are some tricks to the system, but for the most part it's easy enough to learn with some practice. This pronunciation guide isn't 100% accurate, but should hopefully get you more or less up to speed quickly.

·····The vowels

a: When this is on its own or after a consonant, it sounds like "ah," or the "a" in "father."

ai: Like "eye" or "buy."

an: The "a" here sounds a little more like the "a" in "cat."

ang: Back to the "a" in "father."

ao: As in "cow."

e: When this is on its own, it's like "uh" or "cup."

ei: As in "hey."

en: More or less like the English "pen," but with a little bit of "pun" in it.

eng: As in "bunghole."

er: Complicated, but roughly like "grrr." Tongue is curled toward the roof of the mouth.

i: Usually as in "pee," BUT: after a "z(h)-," "c(h)-," or "s(h)-" it is pronounced more like the "ir" in "sir."

ie: Like the start of "yeah."

iong: Like "-ong" below, but with a "y" in front of it.

in: Halfway between "kin" and "keen."

ing: As above.

iu: "Yo."

o: Closer to "swum" or "won" than "whoa."

ou: As in "woe," "go," or "nasty-ass ho."

ong: Lips are more rounded than in English "thong" or "young."

u: "Ooh." BUT: after a "j-," "q-," "y-," or "x-" this becomes ü (see below).

ui: As in "no way."

un: "Would" plus an "n." BUT: after a "j-," "q-," "y-," or "x-" this becomes ü (see below).

uo: Like "won" with a bit of "woe."

ü: Make like you're about to whistle—rounded lips, raised tongue. Now say "whee" or "oo."

ün: Ditto, but with an "-n" after it.

·····The consonants

Consonants in Chinese are mostly the same as in English, though unvoiced. (If that doesn't mean anything to you, don't worry.) There are some unfamiliar sounds, though:

c-: A hard "ts-," like "t's" in "that's it."

g-: Always a hard "g-," as in "go."

h-: Closer to a "ch-" as in "ach" or Scottish "loch."

j-: Roughly like "itch," but without the puff of air. A normal English "j" will do in a pinch.

q-: Roughly like "itch," but this time with the puff of air.

r-: About halfway between a French "j" and an English "r."

x: Somewhere between "sh" and "sy."

z: Like "ts-," as with "c-" above, but without the puff of air. The sound in "cads," "ads," etc.

zh-: Like "judge," "edge," etc. Not pronounced like a French "j."

Finally, Standard Mandarin has something called 儿化 (érhuà; "erization"). In érhuà, an "r" sound is added to the end of a word—remember that this is the Chinese "r," which is pronounced with the tip of the tongue sticking up toward the roof of the mouth, rather than the English "r." Most of the time, this behaves the way you would expect it to—for example, 把儿 (bǎr; "handle") is pronounced as "bǎ" plus "-r." (Although these words are written with two characters, they are only pronounced as one syllable.) What happens to words ending in "-n" or "-ng" is a little less intuitive: in the case of the word 玩儿 (wán; "to play"), the word is pronounced almost as if it were "wár," but with a more nasal realization of the vowel—ditto for words ending in "-ng."

Now let's get dirty.

CHAPTER 1

HOWDY CHINESE

DǍ ZHĀOHU

打招呼

·····Hello
Nǐnhǎo

您好

Back in the day, the standard greeting was "Hi, Comrade," but thanks to the perfidious influence of the debauched Taiwanese, saying that these days will make you sound like a friend of Dorothy to pretty much anyone under age 50. There are many ways to greet people in China, starting from the more formal "Nǐnhǎo," progressing to the less formal but equally boring "Nǐhǎo," and ending up in "Wǒ cào," "Fuck." Chinese greetings cover all the important facets of life: food, what you are up to, obvious observations on what you are currently in the act of doing, and live bulletins on breaking bowel events.

Hi
Nǐhǎo

你好

Hey
Āi
哎

Have you eaten yet?
Chī le ma?
吃了吗？

I've got diarrhea.
Wǒ **lā dùzi**.
我拉肚子。

Have you still got diarrhea?
Nǐ hái lā dùzi ma?
你还拉肚子吗？

In traditional Chinese towns, most families didn't have their own toilets, they'd share communal facilities, and it was common to greet your neighbors as you entered or exited the communal commodes with "Have you eaten yet?" Tasteful!

'Bout ya?
Gànmá qù?
干嘛去？

·····What's up?
Zěnmeyàng?
怎么样？

Whaddup?
Gànshá?
干啥？

Slightly rural-sounding; can also mean "WTF?"

In some of your more relaxed places, people will greet each other with "gànmá qù?" — literally, "What're you doing?" Unlike its literal English counterpart, "What's up?" "gànmáqù" only has one or two variations — e.g. "gànmá?" More generally you can say "How's it goin'?" or "zěnmeyàng?" This is way more flexible and covers greetings like "What's goin' down?" and the equivalent of "How's it hangin'?"

How's it goin'?
Zěnmeyàng a?
怎么样啊？

How's it hangin'?
Zěnme nòngde?
怎么弄得？
Literally, "How've you been 'doing' it?"

How've you been lately?
Zuìjìn zěnmeyàng?
最近怎么样？

Good morning / Good evening.
Zǎoshàng hǎo / Wǎnshàng hǎo?
早上好 / 晚上好？
There is an informal variation on "good morning," zǎo, but not so for "good evening."

Mornin'.
Zǎo.
早 。

Evenin'!
Wǎnshàng hǎo a!
晚上好啊 ！

Night night.
Wǎn'ān.
晚安 。

·····Long time no see
Hǎo jiǔ bù jiàn
好久不见

As in English, the next part of a greeting usually involves inquiring about the other person's well-being.

Been good?
Zuìjìn hái kěyǐ ba?
最近还可以吧？

Same as ever.
Lǎoyàngzi.
老样子。

You're still as fat as ever!
Nǐ háishì zhème **pàng**!
你还是这么**胖**！

Just as retarded as ever!
Nǐ háishì zhème **chī**!
你还是这么**痴**！

Hey, guys!
Hēi, gērmen!
嘿，哥儿们！

·····Goodbye
Zàijiàn
再见

When it comes to bidding farewell, there are also a few variations on the old "zàijiàn":

Bye-bye.
Bàibai.
拜拜。

See ya next time.
Xià cì jiàn.
下次见 。

I'm off.
Wǒ zǒu le.
我走了。

See you 'round.
Huítóu jiàn.
回头见 。

·····Hey!
Wèi!
喂 !

In British English, "oi" is a slightly impolite word used to get people's attention. In Chinese, "Wèi!" is a slightly impolite word used to get people's attention, or to answer the phone. Whatever, if expediency is key then here's a few more useful goodies:

Come here a sec.
Guòlái yī xiàr.
过来一下儿 。

I want to have a word with you.
Wǒ yǒu huà gēn nǐ shuō.
我有话跟你说 。

·····Me
Wǒ
我

In Chinese there are a variety of ways to express me, from me, to me-myself, to the ridiculously formal, sometimes used in jest "Speaking personally, I," to the hickish "ǎn."

I myself
Wǒ zìjǐ
我自己

Speaking personally, I...
Wǒ běn rén...
我本人 。。。

The above two words are usually used to contrast yourself with other people, as in sentences like 现在兽交在上海越来越流行，不过我本人还没这个倾向。(Xiànzài shòujiāo zài Shànghǎi yuè lái yuè liúxíng, bùguò wǒ běn rén hái méi zhège qīngxiàng; "Bestiality is getting more and more popular in Shanghai these days, but I haven't got the taste for it myself.")

Ah wanna go home (to the farm)!
Ǎn yào **huí lǎojiā**!
俺要回老家！

I'm an honest, dependable guy worthy of your affections. (I want to get into your pants.)
Wǒ shì yī ge shízài de, **kěkào de rén**, hé wǒ zài yīqǐ de huà nǐ jiù huì xìngfú.
我是一个实在的，**可靠的人**，和我在一起的话你就会幸福。

·····Sorry
Duìbùqǐ
对不起

There are quite a few ways to apologize in Chinese. From "I'm sorry" to "I do apologize," there are plenty of ways you can say sorry and really mean it, or just shrug when you "accidentally" elbow the guy who's been blocking the subway doors like he owns the goddamned train.

My bad.
Bù hǎo yīsi.
不好意思 。

I do apologize.
Zhēn bàoqiàn.
真抱歉。

A mistake.
Gǎo cuò le.
搞错了。

You're cool?
Méishìr ba?
没事儿吧？

Oops. (Or "Uh-oh.")
Āiyō.
哎哟。

·····Excuse me
Bù hǎo yīsi
不好意思

"Excuse me" is one of those multipurpose words that smooths over a social faux-pas or vomiting all over someone's new leather jacket, or it can be an apology for farting. But if there's a bunch of ignorant fuckers blocking your way and you want to get past, this is the way to deal with them:

Coming through!
Rang yī xià!
让一下！

'Scuse me!
Guò yī xià!
过一下！

Beg pardon!
Láojià lei!
劳驾嘞！

'Scuse my craphouse Chinese.
Bù hǎo yìsi, wǒ Zhōngwén jiǎngdé zhème **chǒu**.
不好意思，我中文讲得这么**丑**。

Sorry I'm late.
Bù hǎo yìsi, chídàole.
不好意思，迟到了。

Aside from "sorry" and "excuse me," there are a couple other slangy ways to shrug off guilt:

You're so unlucky! (expressing sympathy)
Nǐ zhēn **dǎoméi**!
你真**倒霉**！

It's all my fault.
Dōu guài wǒ.
都怪我。

What a pity.
Zhēn kěxī.
真可惜。

You poor thing.
Nǐ zhēn kělián.
你真可怜。

Watch it! (When it's someone else's fault.)
Xiǎoxīn diǎnr!
小心点儿！

Watch where you're going! (When someone bumps into you.)
Nǐ kànzhe diǎnr!
你看着点儿！

Look out!
Xiǎoxīn!
小心！

This warning is especially useful if you're flying on your bike and some dumbshit just wanders out in front of you. This sort of apparent utter unawareness of one's surroundings happens often enough in China to make you wonder how on earth we've managed to come so far as a species.

·····Please
Qǐng
请

Asking for a favor is another of those things that you usually want to be polite about. But when you are talking to friends, feel free to be a little more casual:

When you get the chance...
Yǒu shíjiān…
有时间…

 give me a call.
 gěi wǒ dǎ diànhuà.
 给我打电话。

Could you...
Kě bù kěyǐ...
可不可以 。。。

 lend me 100 bucks?
 jiè wǒ yībǎi kuài?
 借我一百块？

 help get me some toilet paper?
 bāng wǒ ná diǎnr zhǐ guòlái?
 帮我拿点儿纸过来？
 Pro Tip: Most toilets in China do not supply toilet paper and 97% of foreign travelers find this out the hard way. Be smart— bring your own!

 help me scratch this itch?
 bāng wǒ zhuāzhuā yǎng?
 帮我抓抓痒？

Could you give me your name? **Could you?**
Kěyǐ gàosu wǒ nǐ de míngzi ma? **Kěyǐ ma?**
可以告诉我你的名字吗？**可以吗？**

ZÌWǑ JIÈSHÀO

自我介绍

My name is Martin.
Wǒ jiào Mǎdīng.

我叫马丁。

I'm from Nebraska.
Wǒ láizì Měiguó de Nèibùlāsījiā zhōu.

我来自美国的内布拉斯加州。

I've got a terminal illness.
Wǒ shēn huàn juézhèng le.

我身患绝症了。

And, innocent of the ways of the world, I have never known a woman.
Wǒ méi zěnme jiàn guò shìmian, hái méi cháng guò nürén de wèidào.

我没怎么见过世面，还没尝过女人的味道。

Could you **give me your number?**
Kě bù kěyǐ **liú ge diànhuà (hào)?**

可不可以**留个电话(号)**？

I'll join you and your hot friend for the night, **cool?**
Wǒ jīnwǎn péi nǐmen liǎng ge měinǚ yīqǐ kuàihuo, **hǎo bù hǎo?**

我今晚陪你们两个美女一起快活，**好不好**？

I hope we can hang out more.
Xīwàng zánliǎ kěyǐ duō zài yīqǐ wánr.

希望咱俩可以多在一起玩儿。

You should. . .
Nǐ yīnggāi...

你应该。。。

I'm Renee.
Wǒ shì Renee.
我是 Renee 。

I'm from England.
Wǒ láizi Yīngguó.
我来自英国 。

I'm woman enough for two men.
Wǒ de shēncái fēngmǎn dé zúyǐ tóngshí mǎnzú liǎng ge nánrén.
我的身材丰满得足以同时满足两个男人 。

I was born a guy...
Wǒ chūshēng shí shì ge nánháir...
我出生时是个男孩儿 。。。

...but with the amazing advances in **medical technology** these days...
Bù guò xiàn zài **yīxué jìshù** zhēn liǎobùqǐ...
不过现在**医学技术**真了不起 。。。

Let's be **friends**.
Zánmen jiāo ge **péngyǒu** ba.
咱们交个**朋友**吧 。

think hard about what you've done.
hǎohāo fǎnxǐng.
好好反省 。

come kick it at my place sometime.
yǒu shíjiān lái wǒ jiā wánr.
有时间来我家玩儿 。

I'm begging you...
Wǒ qiúqiú nǐ...
我求求你 。。。

I'm begging you, pleeease take a shower, you stink worse than goddamned dog shit!
Wǒ qiúqiú nǐ gǎnkuài qù xǐzǎo, nǐ shēnshàng de wèir bǐ tāmāde gǒushǐ hái chòu!
我求求你，赶快去洗澡，你身上的味儿比他妈的狗屎还臭！

Whether you are sitting next to some over-friendly fella from Hebei on the train or you've been introduced to someone whose contacts will come in very handy on your business venture, "jiāo ge péngyǒu"—"make a friend"—is an all-terrain phrase that will work in any situation in this nation of natural-born networkers.

·····Asking for help
Bāngmáng
帮忙

You'd better learn how to ask for help here in China, because despite a change for the better in recent years, and the fact that foreigners are treated quite well here, many people need to be overtly asked for help before they will offer it.

Could you help me please?
Qǐng bāng wǒ yīxià?
请帮我一下？

Can you gimme a hand?
Bāng ge máng, hǎo ma?
帮个忙，好吗？

In China, your real friends will always do their best to help you out if you are short on cash. As for other favors, your acquaintances will help you with bureaucratic issues if they can as it means that some day (Brando voice)—and that day may never come—they might just ask a favor of you, too.

I've gotta pay my rent at the end of the month, but I'm running pretty light on cash.
Wǒ yuèdǐ yào **jiāo fángzū**, dàn zuìjìn yǒudiǎnr jǐn.
我月底要**交房租**但最近有点儿紧 。
(Don't tell them it's because you spent it all on hookers and booze.)

Hey, bro, I got a small problem—think you could help me out?

Gēmenr, **wǒ yǒudiǎn shìr** gén nǐ shuō, nǐ néng bù néng bāng ge máng?

哥们儿，**我有点事儿**跟你说，你能不能帮个忙？

If you could ... I'd be so grateful!

Rúguǒ nǐ néng bāng wǒ... wǒ jiù huì **fēicháng gǎnxiè nǐ**!

如果你能帮我...我就会**非常感谢你**！

Would you mind looking after my bag for a moment?

Néng bù néng bāng wǒ kàn yīxiàr bāo?

能不能帮我看一下儿包？

Use this with caution, i.e., not on the nice gentleman from Henan who just stuck his hand in your pocket "to put back some money that you dropped."

·····Nice to meet you
Rènshi nǐ hěn gāoxìng
认识你很高兴

This is what you'll see in pretty much any Chinese textbook, and people do actually say it (though it sounds a bit stilted). A more natural-sounding—not to mention shorter—way to say it would be:

A pleasure.

Xìnghuì.

幸会 。

Literally, "a fortunate meeting."

What's your surname, (please)?

(Qǐngwèn) nín guìxìng?

(请问)您贵姓？

Have we met before?

Wǒmen yǐqián jiànguòle ma?

我们以前见过了吗？

Got a light?
Jiè ge huǒr?
借个火儿？

(Excuse me,) do you have the time?
(Qǐngwèn,) xiànzài jǐdiǎn?
(请问，) 现在
几点？

Do you come here often?
Nǐ jīngcháng lái zhèr ma?
你经常来这
儿吗？

Do you want to get a drink?
Yào bù yào hē yībēi?
要不要喝一杯？

How old are you?
Nǐ duōdà ne?
你多大呢？

No waaaay! You don't look it! (It's a compliment.)
Bùhuì ba, kàn bù chūlái!
不会吧，看不出来！

How old do you think I look?
Wǒ kànqǐlái duōdà ne?
我看起来多大呢？

I'm new to China.
Wǒ shì gānggāng lái dào Zhōngguó de.
我是刚刚来到中国的。

I want to make some Chinese friends.
Wǒ xiǎng jiāo xiē Zhōngguó péngyou.
我想交些中国朋友。

What do you like to do in your free time?
Nǐ **yǒukòng de shíhòu** xǐhuān zuò shénme?
你**有空的时候**喜欢做什么？

Can you teach me some fun Chinese?
Nǐ jiāo wǒ diǎnr **hǎowánr de** Zhōngwén, hǎo ba?
你教我点儿**好玩儿的**中文好吧？

I like hanging out with you.
Wǒ gēn nǐ wánr de hěn kāixīn.
我跟你玩儿得很开心。

·····Taking pictures
Pāizhào
拍照

Can you take a picture for me?
Néng bù néng bāng wǒ pāi yīxià zhào?
能不能帮我拍一下照？

Let's take a group photo.
Zánmen pāi ge **héyǐng** ba.
咱们拍个**合影**吧。

I don't like pictures of myself.
Wǒ bù xǐhuan zìjǐ de **zhàopiàn**.
我不喜欢自己的**照片**。

Every language has a word people use when they take pictures—something long, high-pitched, with an "eeeeee" sound in the middle of it to stretch people's faces out into a rictus grin. In English, it's "cheese." In Chinese, it's "eggplant."

Cheese!
Qiézi!
茄子！
Literally, "eggplant."

CHAPTER 2

FRIENDLY CHINESE
YǑUHǍO ZHŌNGWÉN
友好中文

•••••Friends
Péngyou
朋友

Meeting people is easy in China—from classmates who just want to hang out, to chatty neighbors, to people who just want to try out their English on you, Chinese people treat visitors with a friendliness and kindness that—reserved as it may be at times—is truly surprising for many visitors. ... Unless they're Japanese, in which case history is personal and immediate. Oh, and don't mention the Opium Wars, and you might want to be circumspect on the "three Ts" of Taiwan, Tibet, and Tian'anmen.

Stranger
Mòshēngrén
陌生人

I don't care how delicious their **candy** looks, don't talk to strangers!

Bù yào hé mòshēngrén shuōhuà, wúlùn tāmen shǒu zhōng de **tángguǒ** yǒu duō yòurén.

不要和陌生人说话，无论他们手中的**糖果**有多诱人。

Knowing (or recognizing) somebody
Rènshi

认识

I don't **know** him (her).

Wǒ bù **rènshi** tā.

我不**认识**认识他(她)。

Able / unable to recognize
Rèn de chūlái / rèn bu chūlái

认得出来 / 认不出来

The guy hit me from behind with a blackjack and ran off. I'd **be able to recognize** his silhouette, at most.

Tā gěi le wǒ yī mèngùn, ránhòu mǎshàng liū le, wǒ dǐngduō zhǐ **rèn de chūlái** tā de bèiyǐng.

他给了我一闷棍，然后马上溜了，我顶多只**认得出来**他的背影。

Classmates
Tóngxué

同学

After our finals, I went out with some **classmates** and got so drunk that I woke up on a street corner in Tianjin the next day wearing an air stewardess's uniform.

Qīmò kǎoshì hòu, wǒ hé jǐ ge **tóngxué** chūqu hē le ge dàzuì. Dì'èr tiān zài Tiānjīn de dàjiē shang xǐngguòlai shí, fāxiàn zìjǐ chuānshang le kōngjiě zhìfú.

期末考试后，我和几个**同学**出去喝了个大醉。第二天在天津的大街上醒过来时，发现自己穿上了空姐制服。

Schoolmates
Xiàoyǒu

校友

Schoolmates went to the same school, but may be of different generations.

After she graduated, she found a job through a schoolmate connection.

Bìyè yǐhòu, tā kào **xiàoyǒu** de guānxi zhǎodàole gōngzuò.

毕业以后，她靠**校友**的关系找到了工作。

Coworkers
Tóngshì

同事

His coworkers thought he was such a kiss-ass that he might as well grow a tail to wag.

Tóngshìmen juéde tā zuìhǎo zhǎngchū yī tiáo néng yáo de gǒu wěiba, zhèyàng pāi mǎpì shí dòngzuò huì gèng fēngfù xiē.

同事们觉得他最好长出一条能摇的狗尾巴，这样拍马屁时动作会更丰富些。

Colleagues
Tóngháng

同行

I haven't had time to meet up and talk with colleagues lately.

Wǒ zuìjìn méiyǒu shíjiān gēn **tóngháng** jiànmiàn jiāoliú.

我最近没有时间跟**同行**见面交流。

Getting along well with...
Gēn... chǔ de tǐng hǎo

跟。。。处得挺好

He gets along well with his coworkers, or at least it looks that way.

Tā **gēn tóngshìmen chǔ de tǐng hǎo**, zhìshǎo kànqilai rúcǐ.

他**跟同事们处得挺好**，至少看起来如此。

Tight
Cí

磁

Literally, "magnetic."

> Don't worry—I'm **tight** with him. When the cops get here he won't say anything.
> Béng dānxīn, wǒ gēn tā **bèir cí**, jǐngchá miànqián tā bù huì shuō shénme de.
>
> 甭担心，我跟他**倍儿磁**，警察面前他不会说什么的。

Solid
Kàodezhù

靠得住

> He looks honest enough, but who knows if he's really **solid**?
> Zhè rén kànqilai zhōnghòu-lǎoshí, shéi zhīdào shìbushì zhēn de **kàodezhù**?
>
> 这人看起来忠厚老实，谁知道是不是真的**靠得住**？

Flaky, Sketchy
Bù kàopǔr

不靠谱儿

> He's a good guy, but he can be **flaky**.
> Tā rén hái xíng, bùguò yǒu shíhou yě **bù kàopǔr**.
>
> 他人还行，不过有时候也**不靠谱儿**。

> Dude, he got kicked out of Cambodia by the government? That's way **sketchy**!
> Wǒ kào, tā dōu ràng Jiǎnpǔzhài de zhèngfǔ gěi shàn chū le guómén? Nà tài tāmā **bù kàopǔr**!
>
> 我靠，他都让柬埔寨的政府给扇出了国门？那太他妈**不靠谱儿**！

Considerate
Tǐtiē

体贴

My wife's always complaining that I never think about anybody else.
Wǒ lǎopo lǎo bàoyuan wǒ **bùgòu tǐtiē**.
我老婆老抱怨我**不够体贴**。

Friends
Péngyou
朋友

> **At home she relies on her parents; away from home, she relies on her friends.**
> Zài jiā kào fùmǔ, chūmén **kào péngyou**.
> 在家靠父母，出门**靠朋友**。

Online friend
Wǎngyǒu
网友

> **I've got more online friends than real friends.**
> Wǒ de **wǎngyǒu** bǐ xiànshí zhōng de péngyou duō.
> 我的**网友**比现实中的朋友多。

Homeboy
Gēmenr
哥们儿

Homegirl
Jiěmenr
姐们儿

Friend from childhood (girl)
Fàxiǎor
发小儿

Boyfriend
Nánpéngyou / nányǒu
男朋友 / 男友

Girlfriend
Nǚpéngyou / nǚyǒu
女朋友 / 女友

Friends with benefits
Shuìyǒu
睡友

Bang-buddies
Pàoyǒu
炮友

•••••Titles
Chēnghào
称号

It's common in Chinese to address people by their surname plus their profession—sort of the same way as English has "Mayor McCheese," "Doctor Octopus," and "Professor Snape," except much more so: Lawyer Zhang, Teacher Wang (and there is nothing funny about that name), Director Lu, Chairman Mao, and so on.

Mr.
Xiānsheng
先生

Ms. / Mrs. (formal)
Nüshì
女士

Mrs. (generally an older woman)
Tàitai
太太

Teacher
Lǎoshī
老师

Doctor (medical)
Yīsheng
医生

Doctor (more colloquial)
Dàifu
大夫

Doctor (Ph.D.)
Bóshì
博士

Lawyer
Lǜshī
律师

Shifu (general term of address for an older working man)
Shīfu
师傅

Comrade
Tóngzhì
同志
Now dated and used—at least among the young and urbane—mostly in the context of gay slang.

•••••Family
Jiātǐng
家庭

Ever think to yourself, "Boy, I sure wish there were a convenient two-syllable word for 'father's sister's son's wife'"? Me neither—but at some point in the development of the Chinese language, somebody did. Many of the more arcane words have mostly fallen out of use, but even within the immediate family there's a bit more to remember than there would be for English:

Mother
Mǔqin
母亲

Mommy
Māma
妈妈

Mom
Mā
妈

Ma (slightly hickish)
Niáng
娘

Mothers feature heavily in certain more, ah, colorful phrases.
We'll get to those later; don't worry.

Father
Fùqin
父亲

Daddy
Bàba
爸爸

Dad
Bà
爸

Pa (slightly hickish)
Diē
爹

Older brother
Gēge
哥哥

Younger brother
Dìdi
弟弟

Older sister
Jiějie
姐姐

Younger sister
Mèimei
妹妹

Husband
Zhàngfu
丈夫

Hubby
Lǎogōng
老公

Wife
Qīzi
妻子

Ol' Lady
Lǎopo
老婆
Literally, "old woman."

·····Characters
Lèixíng
类型

Poor
Qióng
穷

Rich
Fùyǒu
富有

Genius
Tiāncái
天才

Dummy
Bèndàn
笨蛋

Airhead
Shǎguā
傻瓜

Plain
Zhǎng de bù zěnmeyàng
长得不怎么样

Musclehead
Dàkuàitóu
大块头

Prettyboy
Xiǎo báiliǎnr
小白脸儿

Nerd
Shūdàizi
书呆子

(to) Party too hearty
Wánr de tài fēngkuáng
玩儿得太疯狂

Responsible (mothers love him)
Lǎoshibājiāo de
老实巴交的

·····Regional stereotypes
Fēiwǒ zúlèi, qíxīnbìyì
非我族类，其心必异

There are some things that everyone just knows: that girls from Sichuan province are feisty and totally up for whatever; that Cantonese people will eat just about anything;

that the Shanghainese are prissy little compradors; that Northeasterners are all bruisers with volatile tempers. Like most stereotypes, these are absolutely true. Here's a brief guide to regional stereotypes:

Beijingers
Běijīngrén

北京人

Also known as 京油子 (jīng yóuzi; "Beijing slickers") and 胡同串子 (hútòng chuànzi; something like "alley rats," after the 胡同 hútòng alleys that wind through the old capital), the Beijingnese are renowned for their laziness, their know-it-all attitude, and their cheerful willingness to argue over just about anything. These qualities enabled them to make their marble-mouthed slush of a local dialect the basis for standard Mandarin.

Shanghainese
Shànghǎirén

上海人

No country is complete without a big-city rivalry: the U.S. has New York and Los Angeles; the U.K. has Manchester and Liverpool; China has Beijing and Shanghai, and they hate each other so much. The locals call themselves 沪上 (Hùshàng; "At Hù," Hù being another name for Shanghai) and refer to everyone else as 乡下的 (xiāngxià de; "in the countryside"). The men are known for being more than a bit effeminate, and the women are known for being impeccably dressed, merciless golddiggers.

Sichuanese
Sìchuānrén

四川人

Sichuan province is home to hot girls, hot food, and hot...uh... hot heavy industry investment opportunities. A lot of Sichuanese leave the province to find work—often as "hairdressers," if they're women, or as migrant workers, if they're men. Girls from Sichuan are known for their clear skin, fine features, killer bods and incomprehensible accents; they're referred to as 麻辣屄 (málà bī; "spicy snatch") if they're working as prostitutes, or 辣妹子 (là mèizi; "spicy sistaz") if they're not.

Northeasterner
Dōngběirén
东北人

Hailing from Dongbei, the frigid bit of China stuck between North Korea and Siberia, Northeasterners generally describe themselves as 豪爽 (háoshuǎng; "extroverted,""direct," "fun-loving"), while people from elsewhere in the country typically describe them as "alcoholics prone to violent outbursts" and assume them to be affiliated with organized crime. This is unfair. Dongbei guys make great drinking buddies, if you're a guy (if you're a girl, you may want to carry pepper spray), and they're good to have on your side in a fight. And with their big hair, heavy war-paint, piercing accents, negotiable virtue and square-headed boyfriends, Dongbei chicks are like the Jersey girls of China.

·····Types
Lèixíng
类型

In America, you have your classic personality archetypes— preppy kids, hipsters, nerds, geeks, goths, punks, hippies, backpackers, rednecks. China has no shortage of its own colorful set of pleasing titles.

The Big Spender
Bàofāhù
暴发户

Frequently seen carrying a pleather man-purse, sporting a flat-top haircut and speaking loudly into his oversized cellphone, the Big Spender (literally, "suddenly wealthy" or "nouveau riche") has done well for himself, probably in some grim former state-owned enterprise, and he's keen to let everyone, particularly his rented KTV arm candy, know about it.

The Arm Candy
Xiǎomì
小蜜

Big Spenders will often appear at dinner with young, attractive women who are neither their wives nor their "second wives." These young women are the 小蜜 (xiǎomì; "little honey"—"mì" comes from the English "Miss"), a category that falls somewhere between "piece on the side" and "arm candy," since they're not even necessarily banging the guy they're with. Identifiable by: apparent belief that speaking like a four-year-old is sexy, high incidence of sentence-final interjective particles, age disparity between them and the dude whose lap they're sitting on.

The Kept Woman
Èrnǎi
二奶

Unlike Arm Candy, Kept Women are engaged in serious, long-term relationships, playing the role of "second wife." The men they're involved with frequently not only 包二奶 ("bāo" èrnǎi; "take" second wives), they 养 (yǎng; "look after") them, buying apartments for them, paying living costs, and even paying school tuition for their children if there are any. It's actually pretty stand-up of the guys, until you remember that they're still cheating on their real wives.

The Yuppie
Báilǐng
白领

Often heard before they are seen, Yuppies (literally, "white collars" in Chinese) are the ones in line behind you at Starbucks—they'd never go to SPR or any of the other local chains—dropping English words conspicuously into their sentences, talking about real estate and stocks, and buying cars they can't afford and vacations that will bring them no joy in a sad attempt to fill the gaping holes at the core of their being. Fun game: next time you talk on the phone with a Chinese person, use English for all the words you don't know in Chinese and see if you get mistaken for one of these guys.

The Slacker
Hùnzi
混子

You know slackers back home? The same with these guys. At high risk of being in rock bands and having poor haircuts.

The Busybody
Xiǎojiǎo zhēnjīduì
小脚侦缉队

The eyes, ears and especially mouths of the neighborhood grapevine, Busybodies are small, formidable dolmen-shaped old women with severe perms and flower-print blouses. Having done their bit for the Revolution, they now spend their retirement sitting around the yards of apartment developments talking to one another, observing neighbors' children approvingly and getting all up in people's business. They're not malicious; they just grew up without TV. Literally known as "the small-footed search-and-arrest squad," they can frequently be seen just watching. Get on their good side, seriously.

The Poser
Zhuāngbīfàn
装屄犯

Literally "poser cunt perpetrator," the Poser thrives in his or her natural habitat of upscale cafes and art galleries. Readily identifiable by emo glasses, Buddhist prayer beads around their wrists and their tendency to name-drop whatever foreign writer is fashionable at the moment, they seek potential mates by talking endlessly about how they went to Lhasa and found it so spiritual that they'd like nothing better than to give up their apartment, car and Macbook and spend the rest of their lives living in a yak-hide tent eating nothing but tsampa and drinking nothing but yak-butter tea. Note: may have never actually been to Lhasa.

The Migrant Worker
Míngōng
民工

The unsung, perpetually fucked-over hero behind China's economic miracle, the migrant worker (occasionally 农民工, (nóngmín gōng or "rural migrant worker") leaves his or her horrible little hometown somewhere in the heartland to come to the big city and work long hours at dangerous, low-paying jobs to send money to their family back home. Hygiene and manners are frequently unfamiliar concepts for these guys, and you'll hear city dwellers bemoaning their crudeness, but give them a break and be friendly if you meet them—God knows they've earned it.

CHAPTER 3

PARTY CHINESE

PARTY ZHŌNGWÉN

Party中文

•••••Let's go have some fun!
Zánmen chūqù wánr ba!
咱们出去玩儿吧！

It's a big ol' country, and depending on who you are, where you are and what your purchasing power is, the local interpretation of partying can range from sculling sorghum rotgut out of paper cups and playing checkers outside a grocery store to bumping and grinding (or at least trying to) at a club serving complimentary pitchers of green tea and Chivas Regal to—if you are, say, the former vice-Mayor of Beijing—getting a house out in the suburbs, stocking it up with toothsome young things from Guizhou and spending your weekends ripped to the tits on amphetamines and Viagra and getting freak-ay. From the corner store to the dance floor, from the 24-hour "barbershop" to the Pussy Palace, from sipping and chugging to snorting and toking, there's more than just one Party in China.

Nobody's leaving till we're all fucked up!
Bù zuì bù guī!

不醉不归！

Where do you feel like going?
Ni xiǎng qù nǎr wànr?

你想去哪儿玩儿？

Let's...!
Zánmen ... bā!

咱们 。。。 吧！

get something to eat
chī diǎnr dōngxi

吃点东西

play Mahjong
dǎ májiàng

打麻将

go to a bar
qù jiǔbā

去酒吧

hit the clubs
pào bā

泡吧

sing some karaoke
kāi gē

开歌

The Chinese have more words for singing karaoke than the Eskimos do for snow. The latest and greatest, the yuppiest of the yuppie, is "唱" (chàng K; "sing K"), where "K" is short for "KTV."

get an oil massage
qù yóuyā

去油压

Literally, "oil and pressure"...on certain key pressure points. Well, one of them, at least.

get high

qù hāi

去嗨

Warning: Thanks to the pernicious influence of Taiwanese pop music, "high" doesn't always mean "high." Sometimes it just means "having a good time."

have another drink

zài lái yī bēi

再来一杯

do another line of coke

zài lái yī tiáo coke

再来一条coke

keep it on 'til the break of dawn

tōngxiāo kuánghuān

通宵狂欢

Why don't we...

Yàobùrán zánmen...

要不然咱们 。。。

have a few drinks at my place!

qù wǒ jiā hē liǎngbēi!

去我家喝两杯 !

People usually prefer conspicuous consumption at bars.

play a drinking game!

huàquán!

划拳 !

Huàquán is an ancient, mystical game involving flashing fingers at your opponent in pre-set patterns and drinking if you mess up. Mastery of this, according to ancient lore, can grant immortality, or at least prolonged sobriety.

go fuckin nuts!

chūqù fēng!

出去疯 !

chill tonight.

jīntiān wǎnshàng fàngfàngsōng.

今天晚上放放松 。

PARTYING (IN THE PANTS)...))

Let's...
Wǒmen...

我们 。。。

blow this joint.
gǔn ba.

滚吧 。

rent a woman.
zhǎo ge jī.

找个鸡 。

rent a man.
zhǎo ge yā.

找个鸭 。

pick up some guys.
diào shuàigē.

钓帅哥 。

Literally, to "fish" for some hotties.

pick up some chicks.
pàoniū.

泡妞 。

I need a wingman!
Wǒ xūyào yī ge tuō!

我需要一个托 !

This term usually refers to a co-conspirator when cheating on one's S.O.

I'm gonna...
Wǒ xiǎng...

我想 。。。

schmooze.
rènshi yixiē xīn miànkǒng.

认识一些新面孔 。

hit up the next joint.
huàn ge dìr.

换个地儿 。

·····Kick starting the night

Dìyīchǎng

第一场

What's the word (tonight)?
(Jīnwǎn) zěnme shuō?
(今晚)怎么说？

Do you have plans?
Yǒu shénme fāngxiàng?
有什么方向？
Literally, "What direction are we headed?"

I'm bored outta my mind.
Wúliáo sǐ le!
无聊死了！

Whatcha up to (tonight)?
Jīnwǎn yǒu shénme jiémù?
今晚有什么节目？

Not much, how 'bout you?
Méi shénme jiémù, nǐ ne?
没什么节目，你呢？

Fuck it, let's party.
Qù tāmā, zánmen chūqù fēng ba.
去他妈,咱们去疯吧 。

·····Getting your schwerve on

Kāishǐ zhǎo lèzi

开始找乐子

So you've already had two pitchers of Chivas and green tea, you're feeling like you're the king/queen of the dance floor and you want everyone to know it. You're gonna need some ammo for this:

This music is fucking sweet!
Zhè ge yīnyuè tài niúbī le!
这个音乐太牛屄了！

This place is dead—let's move this party somewhere else.
Zhè gǒu dìfāng, huàn ge fāngxiàng ba.
这狗地方，换个方向吧。

I might as well go home early and pleasure myself.
Wǒ háishì zǎo diǎn huíjiā dǎ fēijī.
我还是早点回家打飞机。
In Chinese this actually means either "this place sucks!" or "I'm really tired."

I/I'm...
Wǒ...
我。。。

> **feel like partying.**
> xiǎng qù hāi.
> 想去嗨。

> **gonna get my swerve on.**
> xiǎng qù pào mǎzi.
> 想去泡马子。
> Literally, "chase horses."

> **having a fuckin' awesome night!**
> jīnwǎn wánr de zhēn **tāmāde shuǎng**!
> 今晚玩儿得真**他妈的爽**！

I'm gonna rock out with my cock out!
Bù gù yīqiè de wánr, zhǐyào shuǎng jiù xíng!
不顾一切的玩儿，只要爽就行！

Let's kick this party up a notch!
Wǒmen yīnggāi wánr dé gèng fēng diǎnr!
我们应该玩儿得更疯点儿！

I don't give a fuck.
Qù tāmāde, wǒ bù guǎn le.
去他妈的，我不管了。

I didn't know this place existed, it's the bomb!
Wǒ hái bù zhīdào yǒu zhège dìfāng, zhèdìfāng **tǐng niúbī**!
我还不知道有这个地方，这地方**挺牛屄**！

Let's go to that park across the road and make out.
Wǒmen qù duìmiàn de gōngyuán **dǎ yězhàn**.
我们去对面的公园**打野战**。
Literally, "conduct field operations."

Let's go for a stroll.
Zánmen yà mǎlù ba.
咱们轧马路吧。

·····Staying in
Jìngyīxià
静一下

Your Chinese friends will feel obliged to take you out every night, but after getting fucked up two nights in a row, they—like yourself—don't necessarily feel like going out, but they'll take you out anyway...unless you make it clear that although you'd love to chug beers and pitchers of green tea and Scotch, even rack up a couple of lines of K, you really need to rest in order to restore your health. They too will sigh with relief. But perhaps you should invite them to chill with you—after all, they have been gracious hosts.

I'm so wasted, I can't go out again—I'll get a cold if I do.
Lèisǐ wǒ le, bù xiǎng zài chūqù, zài chūqù jiù **gǎnmào le**.
累死我了，不能再出去，再出去就**感冒了**。

I'm just gonna take it easy, you want to go for a foot massage?
Jīnwǎn xiǎng fàngsōng yīxià, yào bù zuò **zúliáo** qù?
今晚想放松一下，要不做**足疗**去？

I'm not going nowhere—I went way too hard last night.
Wǒ zuówǎn hāi dà le, jīnwǎn **nǎr dōu bù xiǎng qù**.
我昨晚嗨大了，今晚**哪儿都不想去** 。

I'm just gonna **smoke a few bowls** and chill with some DVDs, wanna join me?
Wǒ zhǐ xiǎng kànkàn dié, **fēi diǎnr cǎo**, nǐ lái ma?
我只想看看碟，**飞点儿草**，你来吗？

I'm just gonna **chill out at my pad,** you're welcome to crash over if you like.
Wǒ xiǎng **zài jiā xiēzhe**, nǐ kěyǐ guòlái.
我想**在家歇着**，你可以过来 。

I'm just gonna **beat off** at home.
Wǒ zhǐ xiǎng zài jiālǐ **dǎ fēijī**.
我只想在家里**打飞机** 。

·····Funny shit
Tài jībā dòu
太鸡巴逗

Chinese people are constantly taking the piss. Different phrases are used depending on context—check it out.

> ... crack(s) me up! / tickles my funny bone / is a riot!
> ... bǎ wǒ lè huài le!
> 。。。把我乐坏了！

> **Midgets**
> Zhūrú
> 侏儒

> **Everything that comes out of your mouth**
> Nǐ jiǎng shénme dōu néng
> 讲什么都能

> **This DVD**
> Zhè zhāng dié
> 张碟

His / her clothes
Tā chuān de yīfu
他 / 她穿的衣服

The way you dance
Nǐ tiàowǔ de yàngzi
跳舞的样子

Your lame-ass jokes
Nǐ de shǎbī xiàohua
的傻屄笑话

The latest 5-year plan
Xīn de **Wǔ Nián Jìhuà**
新的**五年计划**

...make(s) me piss myself laughing!
...ràng wǒ xiào dé xiǎobiàn shījìn!
。。。让我笑得小便失禁！

Stephen Chow
Zhōu Xīngchí (Xīng Yé)
周星驰（星爷）

They always
Tāmen yīzhí
们一直

Your stupid face
Nǐ zhège dāiruòmùjī de liǎn
你这个呆若木鸡的脸
Literally, "dumber than a wooden chicken" face.

The Three Represents
Sānge dàibiǎo de zhèngzhì kǒuhào
三个代表的政治口号

·····Cool shit
Niúbī de dōngxi
牛屄的东西

This shit is awesome, it's off the hook, it's fucking wicked.
We have millions of ways to express awesomeness, but in

China you only need 牛屄 (niúbī; "cow-cunt") which means all of the above.

...is wicked / killer / bad-ass.
...niúbī.

。。。牛屄。

This DVD is awesome.
Zhè zhāng dié niúbī.

这张碟子牛屄。

Chinese police are off the hook.
Zhōngguo de jǐngchá niúbī.

中国的警察牛屄。

That's one wacky up-mop (hairstyle).
Tāde fàxíng niúbī.

他的发型牛屄。

·····Where Chinese go to play

After dinner the question is bound to arise: where to from here fellow comrades? Chinese, young and not so young, hang anywhere from pool halls, pubs/clubs and karaoke to bath houses, massage parlors and Internet cafes... The list is huge.

Foot massage
Zúyù

足浴

You're hammered from a killer baijiu session at dinner, so your hosts may take you to a foot massage parlor to relax—definitely not for the ticklish. These places generally don't offer oil change.

Karaoke (tame)

Kǎlā-OK / K-gē

拉OK / K歌

This type of establishment is the usual choice after dinner, or even after the midnight snack after the club. Most people here will be getting pretty wasted, but these establishments are considered to be wholesome venues—the type you could bring your kids to.

"Nightclub" (the kind with sex, drugs and schmaltz-pop karaoke)

Yèzǒnghuì

夜总会

Your standard yèzǒnghuì is a scandalous den of debauchery. It has a night club, private karaoke rooms and a selection of scantily clad women and men to pleasure you behind closed doors. At some of them you can even score your drugs of choice and get all Chris Farley on their asses (without the heart attack).

Pub

(xiūxián) Jiǔba

(休闲) 酒吧

Pubs have a mostly Western (expatriate) clientele, but there's no shortage of Anglophone locals either. Pretty girls in short skirts everywhere you look.

Club

Dítīng

迪厅

The music is usually shite, but there are plenty of women for hire at the local clubs. Of course the big cities like Beijing, Shanghai and Guangzhou (Canton) have international standard clubs with the latest DJs from all over the world, plenty of fun, not to mention a wide selection of exotic international whores (and man whores).

Pool hall

Zhuōqiú guǎn

桌球馆

Chilled out local pool halls are usually packed in the afternoons, many of them are actually outdoors. You'll find them the busiest just before dinner time.

Mahjong room
Qí pái shì
棋牌室

You pay a fee, you play mahjong, you lose, you leave. Legal so long as you're not gambling real money, wink-wink.

Bath house (with the option of sex for hire)
Yùchǎng
浴场

Many Chinese hosts will take you to the bathhouse to relax in a communal, naked, manly atmosphere, and if you're lucky they organize prostitutes for your added relaxation.

Barbershop
Fàláng
发廊

Ah, the "barbershops." There are legitimate hair salons aplenty, but we're talking here about the ones with no scissors or combs—just lots of pink neon, bored girls, hand lotion and flexible operating hours.

Barbershop girls
Fàlángmèi
发廊妹

·····Booze and firewater
Jiǔ
酒

China offers a wide variety of places, substances and amounts to drink. In bars you'll find all of the stuff you're used to from home. In other contexts you may encounter 白酒 (báijiǔ; literally, "white liquor"), the choice of taxi drivers and discriminating alcoholics everywhere. Some people will tell you that baijiu means "white wine," but don't fall for it. It's usually distilled from sorghum at somewhere between 40 to

60 percent ethanol and 100 percent nasty, with a delicate bouquet of nail polish remover. If you're a guy, you probably won't be able to get out of drinking it at some point, and after a couple shots of the stuff, you might as well just go with it. Here are some choice phrases to help you along on your descent into Sorghum Hell:

Cheers!
Gānbēi!
干杯！
Literally, "dry the cup." And they're usually not kidding.

To . . . !
Wèi. . .gānbēi!
为。。。干杯！

international friendship
gùójì yǒuyì
国际友谊

my homies
gērmen
哥儿们

my girlfriends
jiémenr
姐们儿

the ladies
niūrmen
妞儿们

baijiu
báijiǔ
白酒

cirrhosis
gānyìnghuà
肝硬化

successful implementation of the Four Modernizations
Sì ge Xiàndàihuà de chénggōng luòshí
四个现代化的成功落实

Yeowch, that burns!
Wā, zhēn gòu là de!

哇，真够辣的！

That's got a hell of a kick to it!
Hòujìnr dà!

后劲儿大！

Chug!
zǒu yi ge

走一个

To (explode a) torpedo
zhà ge léizi

炸个雷子

Your typical Chinese drinking sesh combines aspects of the sprint (sipping is for pussies—real men drain their cups every GO GO GO) and the marathon. It is a long, unending slog that tends to leave you with chafed, bleeding nipples. Sometimes you've got to slow things down a bit:

Just half a glass!
Yībàn!

一半！

(Drink as little) as you like.
Suíyì ba.

随意吧。

随意 (suíyì) can still result in standoffs, so keep your eye on the other person. If he hesitates, put your glass down—he's hurting bad, but if you down yours, he will too.

·····Ordering drinks
Diǎn jiǔ

点酒

What do you have on tap?
Yǒu shénmeyàng de **zhāpí**?

有什么样的扎啤？

Draft beer
shēngpí / zhāpí

生啤 / 扎啤

Both of these words for draft beer are in common use. As a
general rule of thumb, Northerners are the ones ordering up big
ol' pitchers of zhāpí, while the epicene Southerners will sit off to
one side sipping daintily at their little glasses of shēngpí.

I will have a...
Gěi wǒ lái yī ge / yī píng...

给我来一个 / 一瓶 。。。

瓶 (píng) is the proper measure word for "bottle," but 个 (ge) will
do the job too, so don't feel compelled to remember it.

Give me a draft of...
Gěi wǒ lái yī zhā...

给我来一扎 。。。

Tsingtao Beer (pretty much anywhere).
qīngdǎo.

青岛 。

Yanjing Beer (mostly Beijing).
yānjīng.

燕京 。

Snow Beer (pretty much anywhere).
xuěhuā.

雪花 。

Suntory (mostly Shanghai and parts southward).
sāndélì.

三得利 。

Budweiser.
bǎiwēi.

百威 。

Corona.
kēluónà.

科罗娜 。

Guinness.
jiànlìshì.

健力士。

Erdinger.
àidīnggé.

艾丁格。

Tiger Beer.
hǔpái píjiǔ.

虎牌啤酒。

Heineken.
xǐlì.

喜力。

Asahi.
zhāorì.

朝日。

Stout.
hēipí.

黑啤。
Literally, "black beer."

I want **a glass of**...
Gěi wǒ lái **yī bēi**...

给我来**一杯**。。。

yellow wine (rice wine).
huángjiǔ.

黄酒。
Authorial opinion is divided as to the merits of rice wine.
It's usually served heated, results in a nice warm buzz, and
despite the relatively low alcohol content—about 10% Alc/
Vol., can be dangerous given how easily it goes down. Most
popular south of the Yangtze.

champagne.
xiāngbīn jiǔ.

香槟酒。

red wine (red grape wine).
hóngjiǔ (hóng pútao jiǔ).

红酒 (红葡萄酒)。

white wine.
bái pútao jiǔ.

白葡萄酒 。

葡萄 (pútao; or "grape") is important when ordering white wine. It's all that stands between you and a snoot full of **白酒** (báijiǔ; "sorghum wine"). If ordering red, though, it's optional. China has begun producing its own wine, only some of which tastes like cough syrup. Following the recent poison-wine scandal in China, we foreigners now have an airtight excuse to avoid engaging in locally produced red wine chugging matches.

Cocktails
Jīwěi jiǔ

鸡尾酒

B-5
Hōngzhà jī

轰炸机

Black Russian
Hēi éluósī

黑俄罗斯

White Russian
Bái éluósī

白俄罗斯

Bloody Mary
Xuèxīng mǎlì

血腥马丽

Daiquiri
Dàikèruì

黛克瑞

Kamikaze
Rìběn wǔshì

日本武士

Long Island Iced Tea
Chángdǎo bīng chá

长岛冰茶

Manhattan
Mànhādùn
曼哈顿

Margarita
Mǎgélìtè
玛格丽特

Martini Dry
Xīnlà mǎdīngní
辛辣马丁尼

Screwdriver
Luósīdāo
螺丝刀

Sex on the Beach
Xìnggǎn shātān
性感沙滩
Disappointingly, this is literally just "sexy beach."

Tequila Sunrise
Rìshēng lóngshélán
日升龙舌兰

Bacardi
Báijiādé
白家得

Bailey's
Bǎilì tiánjiǔ
百利甜酒

Gin
Jīn jiǔ
金酒

Jack Daniels
Jiékè Dānní
杰克丹尼

Jameson
Zhànměichén
占美臣

Jim Beam
Zhàn Biān
占边

Johnny Walker Black
Hēi Fāng
黑方

Rum
Lǎngmǔ jiǔ
朗姆酒

Tequila
Tèjīlā
特基拉

Tequila is sometimes also known as 龙舌兰 (lóngshélán, or literally "dragon-tongue orchid")—the name for the agave plant from which it's made.

Vodka
Fútèjiā
伏特加

Vodka Red Bull
Fútèjiā (jiā) Hóng Niú
伏特（加）红牛

Whiskey
Wēishìjì
威士忌

Single Malt Whiskey
Dānyi màiyá wēishìjì
单一麦芽威士忌

The preferred modality of whiskey consumption among many would-be movers and shakers is to get a bottle of Chivas Regal and a large bottle of sweetened green tea and then mix them together in a large glass pitcher. It's not as bad as you'd think.

I usually don't touch the stuff, but seeing as how you're here...
Wǒ píngshí **dī jiǔ bù zhān**, zhèi huí suàn shì shěmìng péi jūnzǐ le.

我平时**滴酒不沾**，这回算是舍命陪君子了。

I'll drink first to show my respect.
Xiān yǐn wéi jìng.

先饮为敬。

Nobody leaves 'til we're good and trashed!
Bù zuì bù guī!

不醉不归！

Let's get Xiao Wang messed up.
Zánmen bǎ Xiǎo Wáng guànzuì ba.

咱们把小王灌醉吧。

The punishment is three more glasses of beer!
Fájiǔ sān bēi!

罚酒三杯！

China has a glorious 5000 year tradition of making people drink more than they really want to by 罚酒, fájiǔ, "fining alcohol"—that is, making people chug a number of drinks—usually 3—to make up for some offense, real or imagined. There's no way to get out of this gracefully.

•••••100 degrees of wreckedness
Gèzhǒng jiǔzuì chéngdù
各种酒醉程度

I'm getting...
Wǒ gǎnjué…
我感觉 。。。

Last night I got...
Wǒ zuówǎn…
昨晚 。。。

a bit dizzy.
yǒu diǎnr yūn le.
有点儿晕了。

a bit sloppy.
hē dàowèi le.
喝到位了。

smashed.
hēduō le.
喝多了。

fucked-up.
hē chōu le.
喝抽了。

Hang on, I gotta go tap a kidney.
Dāihuir, wǒ děi **zǒuzǒushèn**.
待会儿，我得**走走肾**。

What's up with Xiao Wang?
Xiǎo Wáng **zěnme le**?
小王**怎么了**？

As soon as he gets drunk he starts running off at the mouth.
Rénjia yì hēduō jiù huàmì.
人家一喝多就话密。

Check it out—he's fucked up.
Qiáo tā guàxiàngr.

瞧他挂相儿。

I gotta ralph!
Wǒ yào tù le!

我要吐了！

Get him to the bathroom, quick!
Kuài bǎ tā sòng dào cèsuǒ lǐ qù!

快把他送到厕所里去！

Man, that poor bastard has got no luck at all. Between the booze and the diarrhea, he's running at both ends.
Yā zhēn bèi, hē zuì jiǔ zài jiāshàng chīhuài le, zhèng zài nàr **shàng tù xià xiè le**.

丫真背，喝醉酒再加上吃坏了，正在那儿**上吐下泻了**。

I gotta get home.
Wǒ děi xiān chè le.

我得先撤了。

My old lady will kill me if I spend all night out again.
Wǒ yào zài **shuāyè** dehuà lǎopo kěndìng děi bǎ wǒ kǎn le.

我要再**刷夜**的话老婆肯定得把我砍了。

OK, OK, OK. But after this one I really have to go.
Chéng chéng chéng, hē wán zhè ge **yīdìng yào zǒu**.

成成成，喝完这个**一定要走**。

Drinking games
Xíngjiǔ lìng

行酒令

> **Dice**
> Shǎizi
>
> 色子

Finger-guessing games
Huàquán
划拳

·····Party drugs
Dúpǐn
毒品

For most of the general population, there's not much of a line between smoking weed and mainlining heroin into your neck because all your other veins are closed up. That said, if you're in any big city like Beijing, Shanghai, Guangzhou or even Changsha—to say nothing of Yunnan province, where weed grows wild—the local party people are getting high on way more than just ganj. In some places E, ice and Special-K are more easily available than the herb. If you do get something to roll up, it'll most likely be hash.

Coke is around but not easy to find unless you hook up with some of the business-minded Nigerian gentlemen hanging around the nightlife scene in Beijing or Guangzhou. Just remember that if you get caught with this stuff, simply getting deported means you got off easy.

Weed
Dàmá
大麻

Papers
Juǎnyānzhǐ
卷烟纸

Pipe
Yāndǒu
烟斗

Bong
Shuǐyāndǒu
水烟斗

Stoned
Hāi le
嗨了

Baked
Fēi le
飞了

Totally fucked-up
Guà le
挂了

What do Chinese people think about pot?
Zhōngguó rén shì zěnme kàndài dàmá de?
中国人是怎么看待大麻的？

I heard that ganja grows wild in Yunnan.
Tīngshuō Yúnnán **dàmá** dōu shì yě shēng de.
听说云南**大麻**都是野生的 。

You know where I can score some hash around here?
Zhèbiān nǎlǐ néng nòng diǎnr **mágāo**?
这边哪里能拿到**麻膏**？

Don't you have anything other than hash?
Chúle mágāo nǐ háiyǒu xīnxiān de dàmá ma?
除了麻膏你还有新鲜的大麻吗？

I didn't bring any papers.
Wǒ méi dài juǎnyānzhǐ.
我没带卷烟纸 。

Take some bong rips.
Shuǐyāndǒu chōu ba.
水烟斗抽吧 。

I'm pretty ripped.
Wǒ tǐng hāi le.
我挺嗨吧了 。

Fuck, I'm totally baked.
Wācào, wǒ hāi de bùdéliǎo.

哇肏，我嗨得不得了。

Haha, she's so ripped her eyes are like all Chinese and shit.
Tā hāi dàle, **yǎnjìng mī de xiàng Zhōngguórén yīyàng xiǎo.**

她嗨大了，**眼睛眯的像中国人一样小**。

Damn, I got the munchies something bad.
Wā kào, xīwán dàmá wǒ **dōu è sǐ le.**

哇靠，吸完大麻我**都饿死了**。

Do Ketamine
Dǎ K-fěn

打K粉

Rack up some lines
Guā jǐ tiáo

刮几条

Let's go into the toilets and snort some K.
Zánmen **qù cèsuǒ** dǎ diǎn K fěn.

咱们**去厕所**打点K粉。

Ecstasy
Yáotóuwán

摇头丸

Can I get two please?
Mǎi liǎng kē ba?

买两颗吧？

Wanna go halves? These are pretty strong.
Yàojìn bǐjiào qiáng, wǒmen yī ge rén yī bàn ba.

药劲比较强，我们一个人一半吧。

How come they just keep shaking their heads nonstop?
Tāmen wèishénme bùtíng de yáotóu?

他们为什么不停的摇头？

Ice
Bīngdú
冰毒

Got a pipe?
Yānguǎn yǒu ma?
烟管有吗？

OK, lets go get some tin-foil.
Wǒmen ná diǎn **xīzhǐ** ba.
我们拿点锡纸吧。

Shit man, I haven't slept since...hey, what day is it again?
Wākào, jǐsù méishuì...ai, jīntiān shì nǎ tiān láizhe?
哇靠，几宿没睡。。。哎，今天是哪天来着？

Coke
Kěkǎyīn
可卡因

Lets do some lines.
Zánmen guā jǐ tiáo ba.
咱们刮几条吧。

I am GOD, MWAHAHAHA!
Wǒ chéng xiān le, hā hā ha!
我成仙了，哈哈哈哈！

Rack me up another line.
Zài gěi wǒ nòng **yī tiáo**.
再给我弄一条。

Let's go into the bathroom for a rail.
Zánmen qù cèsuǒ zài xī **yī tiáo** ba.
咱么去厕所再吸一条吧。

I'm not going to be in China long, so do you mind if I just get my shit through you?

Wǒ zhè cì zài Zhōngguó bùhuì dāi tài jiǔ le, kěyǐ **còng nǐ nàr nòng diǎnr huò** ma?

我这次在中国不会呆太久了, 可以**从你那儿弄点儿货**吗?

CHAPTER 4

BODY CHINESE
SHĒNTǏ ZHŌNGWÉN
身体中文

Chinese ideals of beauty have changed over the centuries, evolving from **杨贵妃** (Yáng Guìfēi) , the chubby skank of a concubine who helped ruin the Tang dynasty, to deliberately crippled women with three-inch **金莲** (jīnlián; "golden lotus") feet, to the severely pigtailed model workers of the Mao years, to the relatively normal standards of today. As you may have heard, there are a lot of people in China. Here are some words to get you started making unkind assessments of them.

▪▪▪▪▪The Chinese "beauty"
Zhōngguórén yǎnzhōng de "měimào"
中国人眼中的"美貌"

Heart-shaped face
Guāzǐ liǎnr
瓜子儿脸
Literally, "melon-seed face."

Doll face
Wáwa liǎnr

娃娃脸

She has a kid in school, but if you looked at **that doll face of hers**, you'd swear she was still in college.

Tā háizi dōu néng dǎ jiàngyóu le, kě chòngzhe **tā nèi zhāng wáwa liǎnr**, hěn duō rén yǐwéi tā hái zài shàngxué ne.

她孩子都能打酱油了，可冲着**她那张娃娃脸儿**，很多人以为她还在上学呢。

Willow-leaf eyebrows
Liǔyè méi

柳叶眉

Upward-slanting "phoenix" eyes
(dān) Fèngyǎn

(单)凤眼

She oughtta convert to Islam and start wearing a burqa—**those phoenix eyes** of hers are the only good-looking thing on her.

Tā zěnme bù xìn Yīsīlánjiào, chuān bùkǎ, Liǎnshàng chúle **nèi shuāng fèngyǎn** jiù méi shénme hǎokàn de le.

她怎么不信伊斯兰教，穿布卡？脸上除了**那双凤眼**，就没什么好看的了。

Almond eyes
Xìnghé yǎn

杏核眼

Pouty lips
Dūdū zuǐ

嘟嘟嘴

Whenever I hear about Angelina Jolie, all I can think of are those **pouty lips** of hers.

Yī tídào Ānjílìnà Zhūlì, wǒ néng xiǎng dào de zhǐ yǒu tā nèi shuāng **dūdū zuǐ**.

一提到安吉丽娜·茱丽 ，我能想到的只有她那双**嘟嘟嘴** 。

Small "cherry" mouth
Yīngtáo xiǎo kǒu

樱桃小口

Hot little waist
Xiǎo mán yāo

小蛮腰

I love walking down the street with my **arm around a hot little waist**.

Wǒ jiù xǐhuan **lǒuzhe xiǎo mán yāo** yā mǎlù.

我就喜欢**搂着小蛮腰**压马路 。

Long legs
Cháng tuǐ

长腿

Big and tall
Shēncái gāodà

身材高大

Don't go thinking you're all manly just because you're big and tall.

Bié yǐwéi shēncái gāodà jiù yǒu nánzǐ qìgài le.

别以为身材高大就有男子气概了 。

Bounteous boobs and junk in the trunk
Fēng rǔ féi tún

丰乳肥臀

Protrusions in front, partay in back
Qián tū hòu juē

前突后撅

Killer bod
Móguǐ shēncái
魔鬼身材
Literally, "demonic figure."

> **Blouse filled to bursting, junk in the trunk—she's got a killer bod that'll give you a nosebleed just by looking at it.**
> Kàn nèi nüde qián tū hòu juē de **móguǐ shēncái**, ràng rén bíxiě liú ge bùtíng.
> 看那女的前突后撅的**魔鬼身材**，让人鼻血流个不停。

He / She is...
Tā / Tā...
他 / 她 。。。

cute.
kě'ài.
可爱。

pretty (mostly for girls).
piàoliang.
漂亮。

pwetty (only for girls; cutesy).
piàopiào.
漂漂。

(has) a certain je ne sais quoi.
(yǒu) qìzhì.
(有)气质。

(has) personality.
(yǒu) xìnggé.
(有)性格。

> **Sure, he's not much to look at, but he's got personality.**
> Tā zhǎngde shì bù zěnmeyàng, bùguò **háishi tǐng yǒu xìnggé** ne.
> 他长得是不怎么样，不过**还是挺有性格**呢。

BODY PARTS THEY DON'T TALK ABOUT IN YOUR TEXTBOOK)))

SĪCHÙ
私处

Although they talk about them damn near everywhere else. Chinese attitudes toward the body are relaxed—relaxed enough that you should not get weirded out if the guy at the urinal next to you complements you on your wedding tackle, or if the saleswoman at the clothing store tells you flat-out that you're too fat for the blouse you wanted.

[finger/toe] nail
(shǒu/jiǎo) zhǐjia
(手/脚)指甲

eyelashes
jiémáo
睫毛

bellybutton
dùqíyǎnr
肚脐眼儿

armpit
gāzhiwō
夹肢窝

nostril
bíkǒng
鼻孔

tailbone
wěizhuī
尾椎

foreskin
bāopí
包皮
Literally, "wrapper."

frenulum
bāopí xìdài
包皮系带
Literally, "foreskin-fastener."

scrotum
yīnnáng
阴囊

labia
yīnchún
阴唇

labia [in classical pornography]
ròubàn
肉瓣
Literally, "meat petals."

If a girl's not pretty, tell her she's cute. If she's not cute, tell her she's just **got something about her.**
Rúguǒ yī ge nürén bù piàoliang, jiù yào kuā tā kě'ài, rúguǒ tā yě bù kě'ài, jiù yào kuā **tā yǒu qìzhì**.

如果一个女人不漂亮，就要夸她可爱，如果她也不可爱，就要夸**她有气质**。

handsome.
shuài.

帅 。

easy on the eyes. (a pretty face and nice body)
(girls only)
pánr liàng tiáor shùn.

盘儿亮条儿顺 。

refined, delicate (girls only).
qīngxiù.

清秀 。

sexy.
xìnggǎn.

性感 。

fashionable.
shímáo.

时髦 。

hip.
cháor.

潮儿 。

> **Aren't we hip?** You spend all your time reading
> fashion news or something?
> **Dǎban de gòu cháor de ya,** tiāntiān jìn huā shíjiān
> zài gǎn shímáoshàng le ba?
>
> **打扮得够潮儿的呀**，天天尽花时间在赶
> 时髦上了吧？

·····The Chinese "ugly"
Zhōngguórén yǎnzhōng de "chǒutài"
中国人眼中的"丑态"

Big face
Liǎnpánr dà
脸盘儿大

Square / slabby face
Guó zì liǎnr
国字脸儿
Literally, "a face like the character 国."

Dark skin
Pífū hēi
皮肤黑

Gaunt, miserable-looking
Jiān zuǐ hóu sāi
尖嘴猴腮
Literally, "sharp-mouthed and monkey-cheeked."

Dull-eyed
Yǎn dà wú shén
眼大无神

> **Look at her, all cow-eyed. Big ol' boobs and a tiny little brain!**
> Nǐ kàn tā nèi **yǎn dà wú shén**, xiōng dà wú nǎo de yàngzi!
> **你看她那眼大无神**，胸大无脑的样子！

Four-eyed
Sì yǎn tiánjī
四眼田鸡
Literally, "four-eyed frog."

Squinty eyes
Xiǎo mī yǎn
小眯眼

Flat-nosed
Tā bíliáng / bíliáng tā
塌鼻梁 / 鼻梁塌

Hare-lip
Tùchún
兔唇

Hare-lip (slightly more colloquial)
Huōzi zuǐ
豁子嘴

Pug / snub nose
Suàntóu bí
蒜头鼻
Literally, "garlic nose."

Flat-chested
Fēijīchǎng
飞机场
Literally, "airport runway."

Flat-chested
Tàipíng Gōngzhǔ
太平公主
Literally, "Princess of Great Peace," "peace" here being a pun on "flat" in Chinese.

Spare tire
Jiùshēngquān
救生圈
Literally, "life-saver."

Jeez, that was fast—I don't see you for a few days, and you go and grow yourself a spare tire!
Cái jǐ tiān méi jiàn, nǐ jiù chī chū ge **jiùshēngquān** lái, zhēn yǒu xiàolü!
才几天没见，你就吃出个 **救生圈** 来，真有效率！

Thick, stumpy legs
Xiǎo xiàng tuǐ
小象腿
Literally, "elephant legs."

Short legs, long torso
Tuǐ duǎn shēnzi cháng
腿短身子长

I've got **short legs and a long torso**—a great figure, except upside-down.

Wǒ zhè rén **tuǐ duǎn shēnzi cháng**, tǐng hǎo de shēncái zhǎng dǎo le.

我这人**腿短身子长**，挺好的身材长倒了。

Bandy legs
Luóquān tuǐ

罗圈腿

Thick waist
Shuǐtǒng yāo

水桶腰

Literally, "barrel waist."

Skinny waist
Shuǐshé yāo

水蛇腰

Literally, "water-snake waist."

Unkempt, disshevelled
Bù xiū biānfú

不修边幅

He / She is...
Tā...

他 / 她 。。。

   hickish.
   tǔ.

   土 。

   a hick from the sticks.
   tǔ lǎomàor.

   土老帽儿 。

   such a hick you can see the manure flaking off him / her.
   tǔ de diàozhār.

   土得掉渣儿 。

ugly.
nánkàn.

难看 。

dumpy-looking.
zhǎng de hánchen.

长得寒碜 。

homely.
zhǎng de ānquán.

长得安全 。
Literally, "safe looking."

> **You don't have to worry about her walking home alone at night. She's totally "safe-looking"; nobody's going to bother her.**
> Nǐ bùyòng dānxīn tā yèli yí ge rén huíjiā, méi rén huì fēilǐ tā, **zhǎng de bèir ānquán.**
>
> 你不用担心她夜里一个人回家，没人会非礼她，**长得倍儿安全** 。

"Beethoven."
bèiduōfēn.

贝多芬 。
Homophone for "would score higher from behind."

> **Everyone says the girls at big-name schools are all Beethovens. The reputation is richly deserved.**
> Dōu shuō míngxiào lǐ jìnshì bèiduōfēn, guǒrán **míng bù xū chuán.**
>
> 都说名校里尽是贝多芬，果然**名不虚传**。

·····Other body types
Qítā tǐxíng
其他体型

Big-headed
Dàtóu
大头

Small
Gèr xiǎo
个儿小

Svelte
Miáotiao
苗条

Musclebound (guy / girl)
Jīròu nán / nü
肌肉男 / 女

Stooped
Luóguor
罗锅儿

Hunch-backed
Tuóbèi
驼背
Literally, "camel-backed."

Pallid
Cāngbái
苍白

Hairy
Máomao
毛毛

Scrawny
Gānbashòu
干巴瘦

Bony
Gǔgǎn
骨感

Apple-shaped / Pear-shaped
Píngguǒ xíng / lí xíng
苹果型 / 梨型

·····Toilet Chinese
Cèsuǒ Zhōngwén
厕所中文

Some people will tell you that it's impossible to say objectively that something is "good" or "bad," that it's all a continuum, and that everything's relative, and that what seems bad to you may be perfectly good for someone else. Fuck these people. These people have never seen stall #2 in the bathroom of the gas station halfway between Deqing and Jiaxing, an example of badness roughly on the order of the Holocaust. They live in a state of blissful ignorance that your author, alas, can never hope to regain.

Micturition
Páiniào
排尿

Urination
Sāniào
撒尿

Pee
Xiǎobiàn
小便
Literally, "the small convenience."

Number 1
Xiǎohào
小号
Literally, "the little number."

Tap a kidney
Zǒu shèn
走肾

Wee-wee
Xūxū
嘘嘘

Frequent urination
Niàopín
尿频

The urge to urinate
Niàoyì
尿意

Pee one's pants
Niào kùzǐ
尿裤子

Wet the bed
Niàochuáng
尿床

Piss tracks
Huà dìtú
画地图
Literally, "drawing maps" (leaving behind pee stains on cloth,
especially sheets or a couch).

> **Beijing traffic is so bad, I'm happy if I can get out
> of the car without drawing a map.**
> Běijīng zhè dǔchē qíngkuàng yě tài yánzhòng le, wǒ
> méi zài chē shang **huà dìtú** jiù bùcuò le.
>
> 北京这堵车情况也太严重了，我没在车上**画
> 地图**就不错了。

I'ma go...
Wǒ yào qù …
要去 。。。

> **poop.**
> dàbiàn.
> 大便 。
> Literally, "the big convenience."

> **defecate.**
> páifèn.
> 排粪 。

number two.
dàhào.

大号 。

Literally, "the big number."

move the bowels.
lāshǐ.

拉屎 。

Literally, "pull shit."

have diarrhea.
lāxī.

拉稀 。

Literally, "pull thin."

> **Man, this diarrhea is killing me!**
> Wǒ zhè dùzi lā de kě lìhai le!
>
> 我这肚子拉得可厉害了！

Constipation
Biànmì

便秘

> **I've been blocked up for a week!**
> Wǒ biànmì le yī ge xīngqī!
>
> 我便秘了一个星期！

·····Farting
Fàngpì
放屁

Farting (放屁, fàngpì; literally, "releasing farts") occupies a special space in the world of Chinese expressions. Someone tells you an untruth? That's farting. Want to accuse someone of bullshitting you? That's "dogfart." Want to refer to the release of intestinal gas through the rectum? That's farting too. Just remember, as Confucius did not say: 别人屁臭自己屁香 (biérén pì chòu zìjǐ pì xiāng): The farts of others are stinky, my own farts are fragrant.

Pass gas
Páiqì
排气

Who farted?
Shéi fàng de pì?
谁放的屁？

I just ripped one.
Wǒ gāng fàng le pì.
我刚放了屁。

Silent but deadly
Siānr pì / Mèn pì
蔫儿屁 / 闷屁
Literally, "weak fart" and "stifled fart."

Farting ("Nonsense!")
Fàngpì
放屁

Smelly farts (nasty remarks)
Chòupì
臭屁

Dog farts (bullshit)
Gǒupì
狗屁

Not worth a fart
Dǐng ge pì yòng
顶个屁用

> **I asked you for 300—what the hell good does 50 bucks do me?**
> Wǒ gēn nǐ yào de shì sānbǎi, nǐ gěi wǒ wǔshí kuài dǐng ge pì yòng?
> 我跟你要的是三百，你给我五十块顶个屁用？

...my ass!
... ge pì!

。。。个屁！

Wow, the latest "Star Wars" is awesome!
Wā, zuì xīn de "Xīngqiú Dàzhàn" zhēn kù!

哇，最新的 "星球大战" 真酷 ！

Awesome, my ass! I saw the originals back when you were still wetting the bed!
Kù ge pì, wǒ kàn yuánbǎn de shíhou nǐ hái niàochuáng ne!

酷个屁 ，我看原版的时候你还尿床呢 ！

Fartbasket (a favored insult among the K-6 set)
Pì lǒuzi

屁篓子

You're the biggest fartbasket on the playground.
Nǐ shì cāochǎng shǎng zuì dà de pì lǒuzi.

你是操场上最大的屁篓子。

·····Traditional Chinese medicine (TCM)
Zhōngyī
中医

Traditional forms of Chinese medicine are becoming increasingly popular in Western countries. However, along with this new wave of coolness comes a whole new generation of charlatans. When practiced properly, the doctors will prescribe various concoctions of natural ingredients that are cooked up into a foul-tasting brew. Traditional Chinese herbal medicine doesn't produce an obvious immediate effect, but you'll usually feel a difference by the second day. TCM aims to attack the root cause of your ailments and to boost your immune system over time, whereas Western medicine attacks the symptoms and produces quicker, short-term relief.

Acupuncture and moxibustion
Zhēnjiǔ

针灸

Literally, "needle" (**针**, zhēn) and "scorch" (**灸**, jiǔ).

The doctor turns you into a pin cushion or burns little mounds of mugwort on your body in order to heal you. Sounds creepy, but it apparently works.

Pressure points / acupuncture points
Xuéwèi

穴位

These are the points that are situated on the meridians (**经络**, jīngluò), the lines upon which "qi" flows throughout the body. You may think of these in terms of the points Spock uses for the Vulcan nerve pinch.

Cupping
Bá huǒguàn

拔火罐

They light a fire inside the cup to suck out the air and create a vacuum, then apply it to your back or ass. This creates better circulation of "qi" and sucks out toxins.

Scraping
Guāshā

刮痧

Here they move the cups that are already sucking purple welts out of your skin around your back, creating a scraping effect. This hurts like shit but feels great when you're done—kinda like when you go for the male G-spot.

Tiger Balm
Hǔbiao wànjīnyóu

虎標萬金油

Probably the most famous Chinese herbal mixture worldwide. For headaches, stomach aches, coughs, chest congestion, you name it, a tiny amount of Tiger Balm rubbed onto the skin, preferably on a pressure point, will do the job.

You don't look so good.
Nǐ kànqǐlái liǎnsè hěn chà.
你看起来脸色很差 。

You OK?
Nǐ méi shì ba?
你没事吧 ？

I'm not feeling so great.
Wǒ gǎnjué bù shūfu.
我感觉不舒服 。

I'm feeling pretty gross.
Wǒ juéde ěxin.
我觉得恶心 。

I'm gonna puke.
Wǒ yào tù.
我要吐 。

I've got a headache.
Wǒ tóuténg.
我头疼 。

My stomach hurts.
Wǒ dùzi téng.
我肚子疼 。

It's my time of the month.
Wǒ de dà yímā lái le.
我的大姨妈来了。
Literally, "My auntie's here."

Please stay away, I have...
Qǐng lí wǒ yuǎn diǎn, wǒ...
请离我远点 ，我 。。。

a cold.
gǎnmào.
感冒 。

the flu.
yǒu liúgǎn.
有流感 。

malaria.
dǎ bǎizi.
打摆子 。

a communicable rash.
yǒu **chuánrǎnxìng de** pízhěn.
有**传染性的**皮疹 。

SAR.
yǒu fēidiǎn.
有非典 。

a heavy period.
yǒu tòngjīn.
有痛经 。

uncontrollable seizures.
chōu qǐ fēng lái kě **guǎnbuzhù** zìjǐ.
抽起疯来可**管不住**自己 。

You're very (pretty / handsome), but I'd rather not (get / pass on my) ...
Nǐ hěn (piàoliang / shuài), kěshì wǒ bu xiǎng (zhān / bǎ... guò gěi nǐ)
你很 (漂亮 / 帅) ，可是我不想 (沾 / 把 。。。 过给你)

VD
xìngbìng
性病

gonorrhea
lìnbìng
淋病

syphilis
méidú
梅毒

genital warts
shīyóu
湿疣

herpes
pàozhěn
疱疹

Please call me a doctor.
Qǐng nǐ bāng wǒ zhǎo ge **yīshēng**.
请你帮我找个**医生** 。

Please get me some (painkillers / antibiotics).
Qǐng nǐ gěi wǒ ná diǎn (**zhǐténg yào** / **kàngjūn yào**).
请你给我拿点(**止疼药** / **抗菌药**) 。

CHAPTER 5

HORNY CHINESE

XÌNGGǍN ZHŌNGWÉN

性感中文

•••••Fuck
Cào

From "boning" to "getting laid" and "a roll in the hay" to "making whoopee," the English language offers more colorful idioms and euphemisms to describe "fucking" than you can shake a stick at. From "fucking a cunt" to "frying rice," Mandarin also offers up a "fat" selection of ways to describe the act of fornication. Of course, dear debaucher, you must choose carefully which ones to use when trying to get someone into the sack, and which ones for sharing tales of conquest with your buddies at the bar. So without further ado—let's get our fuck on!

I'd like to eat your "tofu."
wǒ xiǎng chī nǐ de **dòufu**.
我想吃你的豆腐 。
This is a common expression for "I would like to sexually harass you a bit."

Let's go back to mine and...
Āi, zánmen huíqù…

哎，咱们回去。。。

Do you wanna...
Yàobùrán wǒ…

要不然我。。。

All you ever want to do is...
Nǐ lǎoshì yào…

老是要。。。

    fuck.
    cào.

    肏。

Let's...
Wǒmen...ba. (Add this "ba" to the end of the sentence.)

我们。。。吧。

    do some serious fucking
    cào shuǎng yīdiǎn

    肏爽一点

    get busy
    chǎofàn

    炒饭
    Literally, "to fry rice."

    bang
    dǎpào

    打炮

    do it
    gàn

    干

    hump
    rì

    日

to thrust
chā
插
Literally, "to insert."

"Clouds and rain" (a traditional euphemism for sex)
Yún-yǔ
云雨

"Bedroom matters" (a more current euphemism)
Fángshì
房事

Popping the cherry
Jiàn hóng
见红
Literally, "seeing red." In some rural dialects this can be 碰红 (pèng hóng; "hitting red").

Midnight tryst
Chūnxiāo
春宵

This is soooo embarrassing!
Tài diūliǎn le!
太丢脸了！
Especially useful if you are too drunk to fuck.

All smooth
Báibái huáhuá
白白滑滑

Premature ejaculation
Zǎoxiè
早泄

Impotent
Yángwěi
阳痿

·····Penis
Yángwù
阳物

Every guy's got one, and yet the fun bits of the body are a subject on which so many textbooks and dictionaries are conspicuously silent. On top of that, the tendency of mainstream Chinese media to remove any reference to sex, and language teachers' habit of laughing nervously and changing the subject, might lead you to think Chinese people reproduced by spores or something. Of course, that's nothing but poppycock. (Heh.) It's the world's most populous country for a reason: They've got genitalia too, and they know how to use them.

Where did the nasty man touch you?
Zhège **huài shūshū** zěnme mō le nǐ ne?
这个**坏叔叔**怎么摸了你呢？

Touch my...
Mō wǒ de...
摸我的 。。。

Lick my...
Tiǎn wǒ de...
舔我的 。。。

Spank my...
Chōu wǒ de...
抽我的 。。。

Can I touch your...
Kěyǐ mō nǐ de...ma?
以碰你的 。。。 吗？

> **cock**
> jība
> 鸡巴
>
> **donkey dick**
> lü jība
> 驴鸡巴

second-in-command
lǎo èr
老二

dick
diǎo
屌

wiener
xiǎodìdì
小弟弟

pecker
jīgōuzi
鸡勾子

willy
jījī
鸡鸡

schlong (hammer)
chuízi
锤子

tool
jiāhuo
家伙

·····Pussy
Bī
屄

People will likely point out that 屄 (bī) is pretty heavy artillery, language-wise, and it's true—it's about as harsh as "cunt." And gets used the same way, a lot of the time. Here are some softer ways of referring to the holiest of holies:

The Jade Gate
Yùmén
玉门
This is an old-fashioned, literary term.

GET YOUR FUCK ON)))
CÀOGETŌNGKUÀI
肏个痛快

I'm getting horny.
Wǒ fā chūn le.
我发春了。
Can also be used to mean something like, "I'm in heat."

Can you handle my size?
Nǐ méi shìr ma?
你没事吗？
Literally, "You're okay," and usually innocuous.

Give it to me!
Wǒ yào le!
我要了！

No way, here?
Bù huì ba, zài zhèr?
不会吧,在这儿？

Why not?
Wèishénme bù?
为什么不？

All right then, prepare to get fucked!
Hǎo de, zhǔnbèi bèi cào le!
好的，准备被肏了！

Your cock's so hard, **I wanna suck it**!
Nǐ de diǎo tài yìngle, **wǒ xiǎng xī**!
你的屌太硬了, **我想吸**！

Hairy pussy
Bīmáo nóngmì
屄毛浓密
A hairy pussy is the norm here, but if you insist on describing the norm, you can say this.

Shaved pussy
Báihǔxīng
白虎星

I can't take it anymore, hurry up and fuck me!
Shōu bù liǎo le, kuài cào wǒ!

受不了了, 快肏我！

I'm gonna fuck you till it hurts. / I'll fuck your pussy raw.
Wǒ yào bǎ nǐ de bī cào làn.

我要把你的屄肏烂。

I'm going to fuck you to death!
Wǒ yào bǎ nǐ cào sǐ!

我要把你肏死！

I want to drink it!
Wǒ yào tūn xià qù!

我要吞下去！

That hurts!
Hǎo tong!

好痛！

That feels really good.
Tài shuǎng le.

太爽了。

That's too fucking good!
Shuǎngsǐ le!

爽死了！

You're so wet.
Nǐ hǎo shī le.

你好湿了。

Clitoris
Yīndì

阴蒂
Literally, "vagina stalk."

Clit
Sàodòuzi

臊豆子
Literally, "urine-stinking bean." Aww, yeah.

G-spot
G-diǎn
G点

Pussy lips (labia)
Ròubàn
肉瓣
Literally, "meat petals." You will probably not encounter this anywhere outside of classical pornography.

Pussy lips
Yīnchún
阴唇

Pubes
Yīnmáo
阴毛

Love juice
Ài yè
爱液

Pussy Juice
Bīshuǐ
屄水

•••••Tits
Dà bō
大波

Titties
Mìmì
秘密

Bosom
Xiōng
胸

Teats
Nǎizi
奶子

Boobies
Bōbō
波波

Flat-chested
Fēijīchǎng
飞机场

Bitties (little tittes)
Shuǐmìtáo
水蜜桃

Cupcakes
Mántou
馒头
Literally, "steamed buns."

Big Macs
Jùwúbà
巨无霸

Jugs
Bōbà
波霸

Nipples
Rǔtóu
乳头

Milk trenches
Rǔgōu
乳沟

To get breast implants
Lóngrǔ / lóngxiōng
隆乳 / 隆胸

·····Ass
Pìgù
屁股

Anus
Júhuā
菊花
Literally, "chrysanthemum."

Butt-hole
Pìyǎnr
屁眼儿
Literally, "butt eye."

Back-door (sexual reference only)
Hòutíng
后庭

Ass fuck
Bào júhuā
爆菊花
Literally, "to explode the chrysanthemum."

Butt fuck
Cào pìyǎnr
肏屁眼儿

Perineum
Huìyīn
会阴

·····Sexual positions & perversions
Xìngtǐwèi
性体位

If you want to get down and dirty in China then you NEED to know this shit. Just remember, nothing sets the mood like whipping out a phrase book mid-coitus.

Let's change positions?
Yào bù yào **huàn ge zī shì**?
要不要**换个姿势**？

I want to...
Wǒ yào...
我要。。。

Wanna try...?
Yàobù zánliǎr shìshì...?
要不咱俩儿试试 。。。 ？

Have you ever done...?
Nǐ shì guò … méiyǒu?
你试过 。。。 没有？

I like...
Wǒ xǐhuān...
我喜欢 。。。

I'm tired of...
Wǒ juéde … méi yìsi le.
我觉得 。。。 没意思了。

> **titty-fucking**
> rǔjiāo
> 乳交
>
> **missionary style**
> zhèngtǐwèi
> 正体位
>
> **doggy-style**
> gǒu cào shì
> 狗舍式
>
> **cowgirl (woman on top)**
> qíchéngwèi
> 骑乘位
> This is a Japanese-loan phrase; literally, "mount and ride."

hard fucking
kuángcào
狂奅

threesome
sān-pī (also frequently, sān-P)
三匹 (also 三P)

group sex
qúnjiāo
群交

gang-bang
lúnjiān
轮奸

bondage
nüèliàn / SM
虐恋 / SM
Literally, "abuse love."

golden shower
shèngshuǐ
圣水
Literally, "holy water."

female ejaculation
cháopēn / cháochuī
潮喷 / 潮吹

bestiality
shòujiāo
兽交

whipping
biān dǎ
鞭打

masturbation
shǒuyín
手淫

Masochist
Nüèdàikuáng
虐待狂

Pervert
Liúmáng
流氓

Foot fetishist
Liànzúkuáng
恋足狂

Foot fuck fetishist
Zújiāokuáng
足交狂

Be gentle...
Wēnróu yī diăn...
温柔一点儿 。。。

> **kissing.**
> kěn.
> 啃 。
> Literally, "to nibble."

> **petting.**
> xǐ shŏu.
> 洗手 。
> Shanghai slang.

> **finger-banging.**
> zhǐjiān.
> 指奸 。
> Literally, "finger rape."

> **fist-fucking.**
> quánjiāo.
> 拳交 。

Licking the pussy and sucking the cock are usually just described with the same term, 口交 (kǒujiāo; "oral intercourse"). But if you insist on splitting hairs (and getting them stuck in your teeth), then here's a couple of dictionary meanings for your dictionary-loving stiff ass.

Fellatio
Kǒuyín
口淫

Licking pussy
Tiǎnbī
舔屄

Blowjob
Kǒujiāo / kǒugōng
口交 /口功

Playing the skin flute
Chuīxiāo
吹箫

Sucking cock
Xīdiǎo
吸屌

Swallowing sperm
Tūnjīng
吞精

Facial
Yánshè
颜射

Sixty-nine
Liùjiǔ shì
六九式

•••••Orgasm
Gāocháo
高潮

Faster!
Kuài diǎnr!
快点儿！

PORNO)))

HUÁNGSÈ DIÀNYǏNG
黄色电影

Porn is illegal in China. And so are pirated DVDs and jaywalking and unlicensed food stalls.

Porno
A-piàn
A-片

Skin flick
Sānjípiàn
三级片
Literally, "Category III movie"—from Hong Kong's rating system.

"Fuzzy movies"
máopiàn
毛片
From bad-quality VHS dubs, though the term is still common in the digital era.

Slower!
Màn diǎnr!
慢点！

Harder!
Yòng lì!
用力！

Knock yourself out!
Shǐjìn!
使劲！
Literally, "go hard as you can."

Softer!
Qīng yī diǎn!
轻一点！

Not enough!
Bù gòu!
不够！

I want more!
Hái yào!
还要！

I'm there!
Dàole!
到了！

I'm coming!
Wǒ láile!
我来了！

I'm going to shoot!
Wǒ yào shè le!
我要射了！

I've lost it! (… because I'm coming so hard!; female)
Wǒ diàole!
我丢了！

Whoa, I'm gonna blow!
Wākào, wǒ kuài shè le!
哇靠，我快射了！

No way! That fast?
Á? Bùhuìba! Zhème kuài!
啊？不会吧！这么快！

I'm gonna blow on your face!
Wǒ bāng nǐ xǐ liǎn!
我帮你洗脸！
Literally, "wash your face for you."

I'm almost there.
Kuài dào le.
快到了。

I'm coming, I'm coming!
Láile láile!
来了来了！

Where do you want me to blow?
Nǐ yào wǒ shè zài nǎr?
你要我射在哪儿？

Come in my ass!
Shè zài pìgu lǐ!
射在屁股里！

Here I goooooo! (male)
Xièle!
泄了！

That really hit the spot.
Guòyǐn le.
过瘾了。

·····Sex toys
Xìng wánjù
性玩具

They have sex shops everywhere here—just look for the 成
人用品 (chéngrén yòngpǐn; "Adult Goods") signs. No skin
mags or x-rated DVDs (you'll have to go around the corner
from your local computer and electronics mall for those), but
they do stock a range of toys and devices, balms, unguents
and stiffen-up pills.

Do you have a...?
Yǒu méi yǒu…?
有没有 。。。？

Let's try using a...
Zánmen shìshì yòng...
咱们试试用 。。。

condom.
tàozi.

套子。

dildo.
jiǎ yángjù.

假阳具。

vibrator.
ānwèibàng.

安慰棒。

strap-on.
chuāndài jiǎyángjù.

穿带假阳具。

double-dong.
shuāngtóu jiǎ yángjù.

双头假阳具。

vibrator.
zhèndòngqì.

振动器。

vibrator with moving bead.
tiǎodòubàng.

挑逗棒。

pearls.
lāzhū.

拉珠。

cock ring.
diǎohuán.

屌环。

butt plug.
gāngshuān.

肛栓。

Do you like my fingers or your vibrator better?
Xǐhuān shǒuzhǐ háishì **zhèndòngqì**?

喜欢手指还是**振动器**？

Get a hard-on
Yìngle
硬了

Have a wet dream
Mèngyín
梦淫

Beat off (male)
Dǎ fēijī
打飞机

Literally, "hit a plane," possibly from the name of a children's game similar to Battleship. This one is quite funny, because in Taiwan "dǎ fēijī" means to catch a plane. They prefer 打枪 (dǎ qiāng, "shoot a gun").

Masturbate (both male and female)
Shǒuyín
手淫

Queef
Yīnchuī
阴吹

People come in all shapes and sizes...You may think the Chinese a little judgmental by the number of derisive words they have to describe promiscuous women, but they also have a decent selection of ways to describe dirty men.

I'm a bit of a...
Wǒ shì yǒu diǎnr...
我是有点...

You seem like a...
Nǐ hǎo xiàng shì...
你好像是 。。。

Are you a...?
Nǐ shì bù shì...?
你是不是 。。。？

virgin (female)
chǔnü
处女

virgin (male)
chǔnán
处男

dead fish
sǐyú
死鱼

dirty bitch
dàngfù
荡妇

cougar
là shǎofù
辣少妇

merry widow
sāo guǎfù
骚寡妇

dirty slut
sāo bāo
骚包

whore
biǎozi
婊子

dirty whore
sāohuò / sāobī
骚货 / 骚屄
Literally, "slutty thing / slutty cunt."

nasty ho
jiànhuò
贱货
Literally, "cheap goods."

cheating wife
pòxié
破鞋
Literally, "broken shoe"—as in, has been tried on too many times.

callgirl
jìnü
妓女

pimp
pítiáokè
皮条客

minute-man (quickdraw)
zǎoxièzhě
早泄着

horny bastard
sèláng
色狼
Literally, "carnal wolf."

Old men like 'em young.
Lǎo niú chī nèn cǎo.
老牛吃嫩草 。
Literally, "old oxen eat tender grass."

•••••Gay Chinese
Tóngzhì Zhōngwén
同志中文

Attitudes toward homosexuality have taken a number of twists and turns over the millennia. An old story recounts the tenderness of an emperor for a male courtier whom he loved so much that when his beloved's sleeping head pinned down a sleeve of his gown, he cut off the sleeve rather than risk waking the man up by moving it, leading to the lovely classical euphemism **断袖之恋** (duànxiù zhī liàn)—"the love that cut off its sleeve." A later classical term, **龙阳疲** (Lóngyáng pǐ "Longyang's vice"), is rather more negative, coming as it does from the tale of a famous catamite. And until just a few years ago, homosexuality was against the law and could get you fired from your work unit or signed up quick for electroshock therapy. Times are turning, though, and while there's still plenty of prejudice—and the traditional family pressures to marry and

LESBIAN COUPLE)))
LĀLĀ QÍNGL Ǚ
拉拉情侣

Top
yī
一
Literally, "one."

Bottom
Líng
〇 or 零
Literally, "zero." I wondered about this too, until a friend demonstrated with hand gestures.

Pitcher
gōng
供
Literally, "provider."

Catcher
shōu
收
Literally, "receiver."

P
P
P
More feminine half of a lesbian couple. "P" stands either for "pretty" or 婆 (pó; "wife").

T
T
T
More butch half of a lesbian couple. "T" stands for "tomboy," and was apparently originally Taiwanese slang.

have children—the new generation is developing a vibrant, proud subculture and increasingly winning acceptance from mainstream society. Hell, everyone in the government's a "comrade."

Gay man
Tóngzhì

同志

Literally, "comrade." This usage began in Taiwan, but has since become by far the most common term among Mainland gays.

Homo
Bōli

玻璃

Literally, "glass." This is mostly a Taiwanese usage.

Funny story: I once knew an American guy who was a true believer in Marxist-Leninist thought and moved to China to, I guess, do his part for the revolution. He addressed everybody around him as "comrade." The oldsters ate it up; everyone under the age of about 40 got really uncomfortable. Finally one day it hit home when a delivery guy turned pale, sputtered, hissed "**我不是那样的**!" ("Wǒ bù shì nàyàng de!"; "I'm not like that!") and ran away, slamming the door in his face.

Lesbian
Nǚtóngzhì

女同志

Lesbo (more informal, somewhat cuter)
Lālā

拉拉

Bi
Shuāngxìngliàn

双性恋

Hermaphrodite
Yīnyángrén

阴阳人

Shemale
Rényāo

人妖

CHAPTER 6

ANGRY CHINESE

MÀRÉN ZHŌNGWÉN

骂人中文

Yo momma's cunt
Is fat and wide
With planes up top
And ships inside
Nǐ mā dà bī
Féi yòu kuān
Shàng pǎo fēijī
Xià pǎo chuán

你妈大屄
肥又宽
上泡飞机
下泡船

Insults are for the highly skilled, Grasshopper. It's best not to shoot your wad too early in a cuss-off—start small, end big. In Chinese arguments, as in any form of diplomacy, proper escalation is key.

Dropping F-Bombs[1] is no way to argue in China. In fact dirty cussing should be a last resort, to be used only when the situation is hopeless and one has no care for maintaining dignity, or a bloodbath will most certainly follow.

The best and most effective personal insults are derived from knowing someone (superficially) enough to describe their weaknesses in insulting ways—kind of like a verbal caricature painted with poo.

Disclaimer: The words you will learn in this chapter are to be used with care. Remember there are 1.3 billion Chinese people and one of you, and they tend to stick together—that means if you take on one, you'll be taking on everyone in the vicinity. More importantly, you represent all Westerners—try not to make us look any worse than we already do!

·····What the hell are you doing?
Nǐ zěnme nòng de?
你怎么弄的？

The first stage of an argument: Your intonation and word stress will convey your displeasure.

What the hell?
Nǐ gàn shénme ne?
你干嘛呢？

What the? (WTF?)
Zěnme huí shì?
怎么回事？

Are you blind?
Nǐ mei zhǎng yǎn ma?
你没长眼吗？

---

1   Affectionately known as the B-Bomb by Westerners—
    cunt / 屄 / bī → B → B-Bomb

Having established that they are fucked in the head, you proceed with stage two: insulting a person's intelligence.

Psycho!
Shénjīngbìng!
神经病！

You're fucked in the head!
Nǐ nǎozi yǒu bìng!
你脑子有病！

You've got water in your brain!
Nǎozi lǐ jìnshuǐ le ma?
脑子里进水了吗？

Did your head get slammed in a door?
Nǎodài bèi mén jǐ le ma?
脑袋被门挤了吗？

Dumbass!
Shǎgua!
傻瓜！

Idiot!
Bèndàn!
笨蛋！

These last two can be used affectionately, as terms of endearment. These next ones can't.

Half-wit!
Bàn ge nǎozi!
半个脑子！

Fool!
Èrbǎiwǔ!
二百五！

Imbecile!
Báichī!
白痴！

Retard!
Ruòzhì!
弱智！

Idiot!
Chǔnhuò!
蠢货！

Insulting someone's outward appearance:

You're so ugly, even if I shaved my dog's butt and taught it to walk backward it wouldn't be as ugly as you!
Nǐ zhǎngde chǒu bùshì nǐ de cuò, nǐ chūlái xiàrén jiù bù duì le!
你长得丑不是你的错，你出来吓人就不对了！
Literally, "It's not your fault you're so ugly, but it is your fault that you're going outside and scaring people with your ugly face."

These are really superficial insults that are commonly used when you are pissed, but not yet livid.

Look how fucking dorky this jerk looks!
Nǐ kàn tā chuān dé **duō tǔ**!
你看他穿得**多土**！

You...
Nǐ...
你。。。

He / She...
Tā...
他 / 她。。。

is a redneck!
zěnme zhème tǔ!
怎么这么土！

dress(es) like a ho!
chuān de xiàng ge jī!
穿得像个鸡！

are / is too fucking ugly!
zhǎngdé tài chǒu!
长得太丑！

are / is a fat pig!
pàng de xiàng zhū yīyàng!
胖的像猪一样！

You eat like a pig, it's gross!
Nǐ chī dé **xiàng zhū yīyàng** kǒngbù!
你吃得**像猪一样**恐怖！

You are GROSS!
Nǐ zhège rén **tài kǒngbù**!
你这个人**太恐怖**！

Fatass!
Sǐpàngzi!
死胖子！

Insulting someone's uselessness:

You feckless fuck!
Nǐ zhège rén méi chūxi!
你这个人没出息！

Now you are getting worked up, it's time to start slinging truthful insults—and the truth hurts.

Good-for-nothing! / Oaf!
Wōnangfèi!
窝囊废！

Selfish prick!
Zìsīguǐ!
自私鬼！

Hopeless!
Zhēn méi zhǐwàng!
真没指望！

Useless!
Yīshìwúchéng!
一事无成！

You couldn't if you wanted to!
Nǐ méi běnshì!
你没本事！

Stingy!
Xiǎoqì guǐ!
小气鬼！

Tight-ass!
Lǎo kòuménr!
老抠门儿！

Nagging bitch!
Sānbā!
三八！

·····Go to hell!
Qù sǐ ba nǐ!
去死吧你！

Now you are mad, you don't give a fuck, it's time to start being petty.

You deserve whatever's coming to you.
Huógāi dǎoméi.
活该倒霉。

I hope you get hit by a car and die!
Chūmén bèi chē zhuàngsǐ!
出门被车撞死！

Bastard! / Asshole!
Zázhǒng!
杂种！

Whore!
Biǎozi!
婊子！

Punk!
Liúmáng!
流氓！

Pervert!
Sèláng!
色狼！

Sick fuck!
Biàntài!
变态！

Petty Bourgoise! (insulting nickname for the Shanghainese)
Xiǎoshìmín!
小市民！

Beggar! / Vagrant! (Shanghainese slang)
Xiǎo biēsān!
小瘪三！

Foreign Devil!
Yángguǐzi!
洋鬼子！

Peasant!
Xiǎonóngmín!
小农民！

Broke-ass chump!
Qióngguāngdàn!
穷光蛋！

·····Fuck you motherfucker!
Wǒ cào nǐ mā!
我肏你妈！

Now you've gone over the edge, you've exploded and you don't care if it leads to a fistfight. Just remember that you are outnumbered 1.3 billion to one.

Your mom's cunt!
Mā le ge bī!
妈了个屄！

Eat shit!
Chī shǐ ba nǐ!
吃屎吧你！

Stupid cunt!
Shǎbī!
傻屄！

Get fucked by a dog!
Gǒu rì de!
狗日的！
This can also be used as a general interjective.

Fuck you!
Wǒ cào nǐ!
我肏你！

Fuck!
Cào!
肏！
This is as good a place as any to note that the character for "fuck" consists of 入, "to enter," over 肉, "meat."

I'll fucking beat you to death!
Wǒ tāmāde zòu sǐ nǐ!
我他妈的揍死你！

I'll beat you, you dogfucked fucker!
Wǒ dǎ nǐ ge gǒurì de!
我打你个狗日的！

Son of a bitch!
Gǒuniángyǎng de!
狗娘养的！
So few things translate literally. This is one of them that does.

Fuck your grandpa!
Wǒ cào nǐ dàye!
我肏你大爷！

Pussy!
Ruǎndàn!
软蛋！
Literally, "soft-balls."

Your mother's dripping cunt!
Nǐ mā ge sāo bī!
你妈个骚屄！

Your mother's stinking cunt!
Nǐ mā ge chòu bī!
你妈个臭屄！

Try not to use these unless it's a really messy divorce:

May your children be born without assholes!
Shēng háizi méi **pìyǎnr**!
生孩子没**屁眼儿**！

**Fuck your ancestors eight generations back!
(Seriously.)**
Cào nǐ **zǔzōng** bā bèi!
肏你**祖宗**八辈！

May your lineage become extinct!
Nǐ quánjiā sǐguāngguāng!
你全家死光光！

CHAPTER 7

POPPY CHINESE
BŌPǓ ZHŌNGWÉN
波普中文

When talking about Chinese pop culture and its quality relative to American pop culture, it may be instructive to think of cheese. Imagine that Elvis is a wheel of fine aged Asiago cheese, that New Kids on the Block are Kraft singles, that Avril Lavigne is a block of neon-orange mild cheddar you got at the 7-11. Chinese pop culture is Easy Cheese. What with all of the fuss about China having 5000 years of history and all that, people listening to Chinese music for the first time might be excused for wondering how a culture capable of inventing gunpowder and creating some of the world's finest literature and cuisine could suck so bad on the music end of things.

•••••Music
Yīnyuè
音乐

Do you listen to...?
Nǐ xǐhuan tīng … ma?
喜欢听 。。。吗？

Do you know where I can hear. . .?
Qù nǎli tīng…?

哪里听 。。。？

Hong Kong / Taiwanese pop
Gǎng-Tái gēqǔ

港台歌曲

Sappy ballads
Kǒushuǐ gē

口水歌

Literally, "drool music."

Pop
Liúxíng yīnyuè

流行音乐

Rock
Yáogǔn yuè

摇滚乐

Punk
Péngkè yuè

朋克乐

Metal
Zhòngjīnshǔ

重金属

Rap
Shuōchàng

说唱

Reggae
Léigue

雷鬼

Hip-hop
Xī-hà

嘻哈

Jazz
Juéshì

爵士

Techno
Diànzǐ yuè
电子乐

Folk
Mín yuè
民乐

Folk Rock
Mín yáo
民摇

Where do you usually go to see shows?
Nǐ yībān qù nǎr **kàn yǎnchū**?
你一般去哪儿**看演出**？

What bands do you like?
Nǐ xǐhuan shénme
yuèduì?
你喜欢什么**乐队**？

MP3 (player)
MP-sān
MP3

> **Who've you got on
> your MP3 player?**
> Nǐ de **MP-sān** shàng
> yǒu shéi de gē?
> 你的**MP3**上有谁
> 的歌？

**Who's your favorite
singer?**
Nǐ zuì xǐhuan de **gēshǒu** shì shéi?
你最喜欢的**歌手**是谁？

Can you recommend any good Chinese bands?
Néng bù néng xiàng wǒ jièshào yīxiē hǎo de Zhōngguó
yuèduì?
能不能向我介绍一些好的中国乐队？

I said good bands.
Wǒ shuō de shì hǎo de **yuèduì** ne.
我说的是好的**乐队**呢。

This music is truly eye-opening.
Zhè zhǒng yīnyuè zhēn ràng wǒ dà kāi yǎnjiè.
这种音乐真让我大开眼界。

I never imagined there could be anything wussier than the Backstreet Boys.
Wǒ méi xiǎngdào shìjiè shang jìng yǒu bǐ "Hòujiē Nánhái" gèng niángmenr de yīnyuè.
我没想到世界上竟有比 "后街男孩" 更娘们儿的音乐。

·····Comedy
Yōumò
幽默

Chinese comedy tends to come in one of two major flavors: the traditional northern 相声 (xiàngsheng; "cross-talk"), which is similar in structure and humor content to a couple of early-morning AM radio hosts deprived of their palette of funny sound effects, and the more recent, often Cantonese-language *mo lei tau* (无厘头, wúlítóu) comedy typified by Stephen Chow and other Hong Kong comedians, who make Robin Williams on a cocaine bender look reserved.

Joke
Xiàohuà
笑话

(to be) The butt of the joke
(zuò) Xiàoliào
(作)笑料

Pun
Shuāngguān yǔ
双关语

THE GRASS MUD HORSE>>>
CĂONÍ MĂ
草泥马

While online censorship in China isn't the totalitarian affair many imagine, there are some words—especially words of the naughty variety—that get screened out by many forums and blog sites. This post-facto screening is known as "harmonizing"—和谐 (héxié)—a play on the government's stated policy of building a "harmonious society" (和谐社会, héxiéshèhuì).

> My post got "harmonized" by the moderator!
> Wǒ de tiězi ràng guǎnlǐyuán géi héxié le!
> **我的帖子让管理员给和谐了！**

For years Chinese Internet got around keyword-based censorship by substituting homophonous characters, like "river crab" (河蟹, héxiè), a rough homophone for "harmony." People had fun with this for a while, but didn't do much with it until more recently, when netizens came up with a whole menagerie of imaginary, homophonous animals—including the "grass mud horse" (草泥马, cǎoní mǎ), or "Fokk Ewe," a rough homophone for "fuck your mother" (肏你妈, cào nǐ mā). There followed a whole imaginary zoological study of the "grass mud horse" that found that it lived in the "Gobi ass-hurt" (马勒戈壁, mǎlè Gēbì; "Horse-bit Gobi"), a rough homophone for 妈了个屄 (mā le ge bī; "your mother's cunt"), and was engaged in a constant battle for its survival against the perfidious river crabs. This gave rise to Photoshopped, LOLCats-like pictures (with doofy-looking alpacas playing the part of the grass mud horse), online slang that got old almost instantly, stuffed animal representations of the key players in the "grass mud horse" mythos, and an adorable music video set to the tune of the Smurfs theme song.

Retard(ed)
Ruòzhì
弱智

Catchphrase
Míngjù
名句

I'm a **famously unfamous** xiangsheng performer!
Wǒ shì yī ge **zhùmíng de fēi zhùmíng** xiàngsheng
yǎnyuán!

我是一个**著名的非著名**相声演员！

Six **grenades** for a buck—and I've got a hundred
bucks to throw at you!
Yī kuài qián liù ge **shǒuliúdàn**, wǒ xiān rēng nǐ yībǎi kuài
qián de!

一块钱六个**手榴弹**，我先扔你一百块钱
的！

My admiration for you **surges like the mighty
waters of the Yangtze River,** and is furthermore as
impossible to restrain as the Yellow River in flood.
Wǒ duì nǐ de jìngyǎng **yǒurú Jiāng shuǐ miánmián bù
jué,** yòu yóurú Huáng Hé fànlàn yī fā bù kě shōushí.

我对你的敬仰**犹如江水绵绵不绝**，又犹如黄
河泛滥一发不可收拾。

·····Movies
Diànyǐng
电影

Fun project: see how many people, out of a random group
of strangers on the street, have ever heard of 史泰龙
(Shǐtàilóng; Sylvester Stallone), 汤姆克鲁斯 (Tāngmǔ Kèlǔsī;
Tom Cruise) or 阿诺德施瓦幸格 (Ānuòdé Shīwǎxìnggé;
Arnold Schwarzenegger). Then see how many have heard
of 甘地 (Gāndì; Gandhi) or 马丁路德金 (Mǎdīng Lùdé Jīn;
Martin Luther King).

Action
Dòngzuò piān
动作片

Kung-fu
Wǔdǎ piān
武打片

Sci-fi
Kē-huàn piān
科幻片

Horror
Kǒngbù piān
恐怖片

Suspense
Xuánniàn piān
悬念片

Romance
Làngmàn piān
浪漫片

I like movies with...
Wǒ xǐhuan diànyǐng yǒu …
我喜欢电影有 。。。

    historical significance.
    lìshǐ yìyì.
    历史意义 。

artistic value.
yìshù jiàzhí.
艺术价值 。

intricately realized characters.
xìnì fùzá de **rénwù** miáoxiě.
细腻复杂的**人物**描写 。

explosions and tits.
bàozhà hé dà bō.
爆炸和大波 。

·····Fashion
Shíshàng
时尚

Japanese-style
Rì fànr
日范儿

"Japanese-style" is a catchall term for the gallimaufry of sartorial oddities imported from China's neighbor to the east, from Visual Kei (视觉系 , shìjué xì), the bastard offspring of anime and hair metal favored by Japanese goths, to more generally J-Pop–influenced looks.

Lolita
Luòlìtǎ
洛丽塔

Lolitas come in two flavors: monochrome and Technicolor. In both cases, frills and flounces play an important role; in the latter case, so does hot pink.

Cosplay
(Just "cosplay.")
The good news: Yes, there really are girls who dress up like Chun Li and Sailor Moon. The bad news: they're still, physically, the kind of people who tend to be really into Chun Li and Sailor Moon.

Kawai
Kǎwāyī

卡哇伊

Named after the Japanese word for "cute," Kawai tends to be coincident with terminal cases of 嗲 (diǎ), a neurological disorder that causes young and occasionally not-so-young women to believe that acting like a four-year-old is sexy.

Korean-style
Hán fànr

韩范儿

Clothes copied from whatever Korean soap opera is popular at the moment. Can range from relatively inoffensive—blue jeans, sneakers, baseball caps, cute suit jackets on girls—to full-on bleached-hair FUBU breakdancing hilarity.

English-style
Yīng fànr

英范儿

Burberry and Burberry knock-offs. As dull as its namesake country.

His / Her outfit looks (really…)
Tā chuānde (fēicháng)…

他 / 她穿得非常 。。。

retro.
fùgǔ.

复古 。

avante-garde.
qiánwèi.

前卫 。

stylish.
shímáo.

时髦 。

cute.
kěài.

可爱 。

like a model.
xiàng mòtèr.

像模特儿 。

lame.
tǔ.

土 。

slutty.
lòu.

露 。
Literally, "revealing."

hideous.
xiàrén.

吓人 。
Literally, "frightening."

CHAPTER 8

SPORTY CHINESE
JÌNGJÌ ZHŌNGWÉN
竞技中文

Chinese are crazy about sports. More and more elite Chinese athletes and sports people are becoming internationally recognized household faces. If you can talk sports in Chinese, you'll make a lot of friends.

Do you like to... ?
Nǐ xǐhuan … ma?
你喜欢 。。。吗？

I want to ...
Wǒ xiǎng …
我想 。。。

play soccer.
tī zúqiú.
踢足球 。
Here 踢 (tī; "kick") means play.

play basketball.
dǎ lánqiú.
打篮球 。
Here 打 (dǎ; "hit") means play.

play baseball.
dǎ bàngqiú.

打棒球。

play (beach) volleyball.
dǎ (shātān) páiqiú.

打 (沙滩) 排球。

play badminton.
dǎ yǔmáoqiú.

打羽毛球。

Not only is badminton actually considered a sport in China, but it's incredibly popular. You'll see people playing it out in the street when the weather's warm.

play ping-pong.
dǎ pīngpāng.

打乒乓。

play tennis.
dǎ wǎngqiú.

打网球。

play ice hockey.
dǎ bīngqiú.

打冰球。

A SOCCER JOKE)))

God decided to have a soccer match with the devil.
Shàngdì juédìng hé Sādàn jǔxíng yī chǎng zúqiúsài.

上帝决定和撒旦举行一场足球赛。

God said to **the devil**, "I've got this thing sewn up—all the best players are on my side."
Shàngdì duì **Sādàn** shuō, "Wǒ yíng dìng le, yīnwèi wǒ yōngyǒu shìjiè shang zuì hǎo de qiúyuán."

上帝对**撒旦**说："我赢定了，因为我拥有世界上最好的球员。"

"Don't be so sure," said the devil. "I've got a **Chinese ref**."
Sādàn huídá, "Nǐ bié gāoxìng tài zǎo le, wǒ qǐng de shì **Zhōngguó cáipàn**."

撒旦回答："你别高兴太早了，我请的是**中国裁判**。"

play field hockey.
dǎ qūgùnqiú.

打曲棍球。

play mahjong.
dǎ májiàng.

打麻将。

Combining the nail-biting excitement of dominoes with the gambler-crack addictiveness of poker, mahjong was banned by the new Chinese government in 1949, but legalized again once they realized there was no getting rid of it. Every region of China has its own variant of mahjong, so if you get accused of cheating and/or incompetence, just say you're playing by an obscure set of rules from another part of the country and no one will be the wiser.

Hey, I win!
Hú le!

胡了！

Well, I **almos**t won, anyway.
Fǎnzheng shì **chàdiǎn** hú le.

反正是**差点**胡了。

According to Inner Mongolian rules, at least.
Zhìshǎo shì ànzhào Nèi Měng de **chángguī**.
至少是按照内蒙的**常规**。

I don't play sports, but I like to watch.
Wǒ bùzěnme yùndong, kě xǐhuān kàn bǐsài.
不怎么运动，可喜欢看比赛。

Especially women's beach volleyball.
Tèbié shi nǚzǐ shātān páiqiú.
特别是女子沙滩排球。

What...do you like?
Nǐ xǐhuan shénme …?
你喜欢什么。。。？

sports
yùndong
运动

teams
qiúduì
球队

players
yùndòngyuán
运动员

·····Other sports and games
Qíta yùndòng hé yóuxì
其他运动和游戏

Billiards
Zhuōqiú
桌球

Billiards
Táiqiú
台球

Chess
Guójì xiàngqí
国际象棋

Go
Wéiqí
围棋

Bowling
Bǎolíngqiú
保龄球

Darts
Fēibiāo
飞镖

Rugby
Gǎnlǎnqiú
橄榄球

American football
Měishì gǎnlǎnqiú
美式橄榄球

Golf
Gāo'ěrfū
高尔夫

•••••Cheering and jeering
Hècǎi yǔ hèdàocǎi
喝彩与喝倒彩

Go, ...!
...jiāyóu!
。。。加油！

We support you!
Wǒmen **zhīchí** nǐ!
我们**支持** 你！

Kick-ass!
Niúbī!
牛屄！
Literally, "cow-cunt."

Which (ball) team do you support?
Nǐ zhīchí něige qiúduì?
你支持哪个球队？

Not long ago a few young no-goodniks in Beijing formed the Beijing Profanity Alliance (**京骂联盟**, Jīngmà Liánméng), a volunteer organization dedicated to promoting awareness of Beijing's unique linguistic heritage by yelling "THE REF IS A STUPID CUNT" at visiting teams.

The…is a stupid cunt!
…shì ge shǎ bī!
。。。是个傻屄！

referee
cáipàn
裁判

goalie
shǒumén de
守门的

striker
qiánfēng
前锋

·····Working out
Jiànshēn
健身

Many cities provide public fitness equipment—picture the crappy plastic swing sets you get in parks back home, except made of hard, cold, pointy metal and less fun. If that's not your style, or if you're just unable to dislodge the old ladies from the weird clothes rack–looking thing, here are some words that should stand you in good stead at the nearest gym (**健身房**, jiànshēnfáng):

Stretching
Shēnzhǎn
伸展

Leg lifts
Tī tuǐ
踢腿

Jogging
Pǎobù
跑步

Treadmill
Pǎobù qì
跑步器

Weight-lifting
Jǔzhòng
举重

Yoga
Yújiā
瑜伽

Splits
Pǐtuǐ
劈腿

Swimming
Yóuyǒng
游泳

Aerobics
Jiànshēncāo
健身操

Jumping jacks
Kāihé tiào
开合跳

Sit-ups
Yǎngwò qǐzuò
仰卧起坐

Push-ups
Fǔwòchēng
俯卧撑

Pull-ups
Yǐntǐ xiàngshàng
引体向上

I want to work out my...
Wǒ xiǎng liàn liàn wǒ de…
我想练练我的 。。。

biceps.
èrtóujī.
二头肌 。

triceps.
sāntóu jī.
三头肌 。

pecs.
xiōngjī.
胸肌 。

abs.
fùjī.
腹肌 。

gluteus.
túnjī.
臀肌 。

thighs.
dàtuǐ.
大腿 。

calves.
xiǎotuǐ.
小腿 。

(gym) Membership card
(jiànshēnfáng) Huìyuán kǎ
(健身房) 会员卡

·····Video games
Diànyóu
电游

Video games may have arrived late here compared to the U.S. and Japan, but the benighted young people of China are doing their absolute damnedest to make up the gap in hours logged. A lot of gaming takes place online, either through personal computers or at Internet cafes.

Sony PlayStation / PSP
Suǒní PS / PSP
索尼 PS / PSP

Nintendo (Wii)
Rèntiāntáng (Wii)
任天堂 (Wii)

X-Box (360)
X-Box (Sān-liù-líng)
X-Box (360)

Online game
Wǎngyóu
网游

Casual game
Xiūxián yóuxì
休闲游戏

(MMO)RPG
(dàxíng duō rén zàixiàn) Juésè bànyǎn yóuxì
(大型多人在线) 角色扮演游戏
Most people just use the English abbreviation.

World of Warcraft
Móguǐ Shìjiè
魔鬼世界

Dungeon & Fighter (a popular Korean game)
Dìxià Chéng yǔ Yǒngshì
地下城与勇士

Yulgang (another Korean game)
Rèxuè Jiānghú
热血江湖

Counter-Strike
Fǎn-kǒng Jīngyīng (or just CS)
反恐精英

Starcraft
Xīngjì Zhēngbà
星际争霸

Gamer
Wánjiā
玩家

N00b
Xīnshǒu
新手

Camping
Yīnrén
阴人

Head-shot
Bào tóu
爆头

Fire in the hole!
Xiǎoxīn shǒuléi!
小心手雷！

Rush
Kuàigōng
快攻

Dude, Xiao Wang's totally addicted to online games.
Wǒ kào, Xiǎo Wáng zhēnshi wánr wǎngyóu shàngyǐn le.
我靠，小王真是玩儿网游上瘾了。

What makes you say that?
Nǐ zěnme zhīdao？
你怎么知道？

He's wearing a **catheter** and hasn't left the Internet
café in a week.
Tā dōu zhuāngshàng **dǎoniàoguǎn** le, zhěngzhěng yī ge
xīngqī méi líkāi wǎngbā.
他都装上**导尿管**了，整整一个星期没离开
网吧。

CHAPTER 9

HUNGRY CHINESE
YǏNSHÍ ZHŌNGWÉN
饮食中文

Food is of paramount importance to the Chinese. It's rare that you'll bump into someone you know and NOT ask them if they've eaten yet. If you're on a trip and unsure what souvenir to bring back for your Chinese buddies, just buy some edible local specialty and you're set. They love food so much here, they extended their borders just so the map of China would be shaped like a chicken.

First-time visitors to China often worry about food poisoning. They soon learn that like death and taxes, food poisoning is basically inevitable. After a few meals, though, they're well on their way to having bowels of steel—provided they don't drink the tap water.

Tummy
Dùzi
肚子

My tummy is...
Wǒ dùzi...
我肚子。。。

growling.
jiào le.
叫了。

famished.
è huài le.
饿坏了。

starving.
è sǐ le.
饿死了。

full.
bǎo le.
饱了。

stuffed.
chēngsǐ le.
撑死了。

(My) stomach hurts.
(Wǒ de) wèi téng.
(我的)胃疼。

•••••Food
Fàn
饭

The Chinese have multiple names for rice. It plays such an important role in Chinese gastronomy that cooked rice is synonymous with food in general. The weirdest thing is that when you've stuffed yourself full with all the awesome food laid out on the table in front of you, you'll be asked what you'd like for your main meal. And you thought you'd already stuffed yourself enough for five main meals! The Chinese believe that unless you eat rice or other staples such as noodles or dumplings, you can't actually feel fully satisfied. For them, the staples are the main meal, everything else is just condiments.

The basics:

Rice (cooked)
Mǐfàn
米饭

White rice (cooked)
Bái (mǐ) fàn
白 (米) 饭

Noodles
Miàntiáo
面条

Dumplings
Jiǎozi
饺子

I'd like some...
Wǒ lái diǎnr...
我来点儿 。。。

    food.
    shíwù.
    食物 。

    snacks.
    língshí.
    零食 。

Have you eaten yet?
Chīfàn le méiyǒu?
吃饭了没有 ？

You eaten?
Chī le méiyǒu?
吃了没有 ？

I want to EAT!
Wǒ yào chī fàn!
我要吃饭 ！

I love...
Wǒ hěn xǐhuān chī...
我很喜欢吃 。 。 。

What do you feel like eating?
Nǐ xiǎng chī shénme?
你想吃什么？

What's your favorite food?
Nǐ zuì xǐhuān chī shénme?
你最喜欢吃什么？

How 'bout I make you some...?
Wǒ lái gěi nǐ zuò diǎn...chī ba.
我来给你做点 。 。 。 吃吧 。

I feel like eating junk food.
Wǒ xiǎng chī **lājī shípǐn**.
我想吃**垃圾食品** 。

Let's get some take out delivered.
Zánmen diǎn **wàimài** ba.
咱们点**外卖**吧 。

•••••Hurry up!
Kuài yī diǎn!
快一点！

Because the most common dishes in China are pretty quick to prepare, most Chinese have become accustomed to getting their meals pretty damn quick. So don't be surprised when you hear people everywhere in every restaurant screaming at the waiter to tell the cook to hurry the fuck up. You don't tip here, so don't expect the wait staff to bend over backward to give you good service. In fact, the wages are pretty low, so if you get a smile, you're already doing pretty good.

Waiter / Waitress...
Fúwùyuán…

务员 。。。

Note that it's safest, especially in Northern China, to address the waitress with the gender-neutral term 服务员 (fúwùyuán) rather than 小姐 (xiǎojiě, "Miss") as is common in the south. You see, besides meaning "Miss," 小姐 (xiǎojiě) is also a relatively common term for a bar girl. It depends on who's speaking, and it's no longer as touchy as it used to be, but if you drop a 小姐 (xiǎojiě) up north, you may offend.

we want **to order!**
wǒmen xiǎng **diǎn cài**!

服务员！我们想点菜！

Follow the pattern: call out for the wait staff in a loud voice, then make your request.

what do you **recommend** (to eat)?
nǐ **tuījiàn** (chī diǎnr) shénme?

你推荐(吃点儿)什么？

how much does this cost?
zhè ge duōshǎo qiàn?

这个多少钱？

are the **portions** large?
cài liàng duō bù duō?

菜量多不多？

what is this shit?
zhè shì shénme gǒushǐ?

这是什么狗屎？

I'll have one of these.
lái yī fèn ba.

来一份吧 。

this tastes **strange**.
wèidào **bù zhèngcháng**.

味道不正常 。

CRFÉS
KĀFĒIDIÀN
咖啡店

Although tea houses are the traditional "cafés," the Chinese have caught on to sipping their tea at coffeeshops. Actually, coffee culture is huge here—but as a rule, it's post-Starbucks café culture, not the Old World incubator of ideas/information exchange.

Starbucks
Xīngbākè
星巴克

These are everywhere in China, even at one point (though no longer) in the Forbidden City. Expect no surprises. The clientele are mostly wannabe young Chinese professionals, brand-conscious Taiwanese, and Korean housewives.

SPR (Shanzhai Starbucks)
P
SPR

These "Shanzhai Starbucks" are popping up all over China like mushrooms after a spring rain. The logo looks like Starbucks, the coffee is cheaper and they have free wi-fi—'nuff said. The clientele either come because of brand recognition (albeit the wrong brand) or because they are Westerners who have lived here long enough to know that anything "Shanzhai" is cool (counter-culture-cum-mainstream) and they want to be cool too. Either that, or they just prefer the cheaper coffee.

I can't use chopsticks. Do you have a knife and fork?
Wǒ bù huì yòng **kuàizi**. Yǒu méi yǒu **dāochā**?
我不会用**筷子** 。 有没有**刀叉** ？

Could I trouble you to...
Máfan nǐ…
麻烦你 。 。 。

bring me a menu please?
bǎ **càidān** náguòlái, hǎo ba?
把**菜单**拿过来 ， 好吧 ？

You know how there are some restaurants where they've got "atmosphere" and thick, sound-cancelling carpets and you feel like you have to whisper your order so people don't look at you funny? Most restaurants aren't like that, and a lot of the time you'll probably have to bellow to make yourself heard. This is hard for some people to get used to when they first arrive, but eventually hunger wins out over manners.

gimme a menu!
càidān!
菜单！

leave out the MSG. (It's rare that they'll listen, but say it if it makes you feel better…)
bié fàng wèijīng.
别放味精 。

please bring us some more hot (boiled) water?
zài lái diǎn **bái kāishuǐ**.
再来点**白开水** 。

hurry up!
kuàidiǎnr a!
快点儿啊！

What time do you finish work?
Nǐ jǐ diǎn **xiàbān**?
你几点**下班**？

·····Tasty
Hǎo chī
好吃

This is delicious!
Fēicháng hǎochī!
非常好吃！

Really fucking amazing!
Zhēn tāmā de hǎo chī!
真他妈的好吃！

It melts in my mouth.
Rù kǒu jí róng.
入口即溶 。

This smells awesome!
Hǎo xiāng!
好香！

This is seriously nom-tastic!
Māde, zhè ge cài tēi hǎo chī le!
妈的，这个菜忒好吃了！

Can I get seconds?
Zài jiā yi diǎn hǎo ba?
再加一点好吧？

You snarfed that down like a pig.
Chī dé xiàng zhū yīyàng.
吃得像猪一样。

You downed that pretty fast.
Nǐ chī de tài kuài.
你吃得太快。

Expect to have Chinese friends, coworkers and bystanders advising you on proper eating speed, the health benefits of hot water (热水, rèshuǐ) and boiled hot water (开水, kāishuǐ) over the stomach cancer (胃癌, wèiái)–causing ice water (冰水, bīngshuǐ) Westerners like to drink, and the need to eat more (多吃点儿, duō chī diǎnr) like the Jewish mother you never had.

·····International cuisine
Guójì měishí
国际美食

We've already established that food is the pillar of existence in China. These people have been coming up with new ways to eat shit for millennia. Although they can have some pretty weird ideas of what tastes good, there's so much variety here you'll find plenty of good eats—whatever your tastes.

Indian food
Yìndù cài
印度菜

Curry
Gālí

咖喱

We all know that curry is a combination of spices, and what passes for curry in China is a generic yellow powder not unlike Japanese curry. Never fear: authentic Indian cuisine is becoming more common in China, and any major city should have passable Indian restaurants.

Italian food
Yìdàlì cài

意大利菜

Spaghetti
Yìdàlì miàn

意大利面

Literally, "Italian noodles." The fact that spaghetti—usually spaghetti bolognaise—represents "Italian noodles" indicates that the average Zhang doesn't know much about real Italian pasta. Although you can more or less scratch an itch by eating "Italian noodles" at most Chinese-style Western restaurants, expect it to be about on a par, authenticity-wise, with the Kung Pao chicken you'd get at an Italian restaurant.

Thai food
Tàiguó cài

泰国菜

Thai is available in big Chinese cities, but most Thai restaurants have Chinese chefs and Chinese owners, and stick to bland versions of the standards.

Japanese food
Rìběncài / Rìběn liàolǐ

日本菜 / 日本料理

There are plenty of real Japanese restaurants in China, but the numerous RMB 150 all you can eat and drink Teppanyaki buffets are by far the most popular among locals and expats alike.

Korean food
Hánguó cài / Hánguó liàolǐ

韩国菜 / 韩国料理

Like Japanese food, Korean restaurants exist in every Chinese city with a decent-sized Korean population. A lot of Korean BBQs are run by ethnically Korean Chinese, sometimes with North Korean staff.

·····Fast food
Kuàicān
快餐

All the usual suspects can be found in every major and not so major city. It's not unusual to see multiple McDonalds, KFCs and Pizza Huts on a single intersection in busy shopping areas in huge cities like Beijing and Shanghai. If you didn't have sensory overload yet, you will when you notice all the Chinese fast food joints doing huge business right alongside the global players.

China has its own knock-off (山寨, shānzhài) imitations of the major International chains, sometimes with names like McKFC (麦肯鸡, Màikěnjī); these are usually crap, but some are even better than the originals. Chinese fast food chains serve up huge selections of local (fast) food—fast even by the generally zippy standards of Chinese restaurants.

Let's go to...
Zánmen qù...chīfàn ba.
咱们去…吃饭吧 。

Kung-Fu
Zhēn Gōngfu
真功夫
You can't miss these Kung-Fu stores—they've got big red signs with a black and yellow picture of someone who their lawyers swear is not Bruce Lee. They claim to be the healthiest fast food choice in China, as the food is all steamed—noodles, pork ribs, vegetables, etc. Why call it Kung-Fu? Could be that 真功夫 (Zhēn Gōngfu) sounds like 蒸功夫 (zhēng gōngfu; steam power), but way cooler.

Yonghe Dawang
Yǒnghé Dàwáng
永和大王
These are everywhere in China and are inexplicably popular. The noodles are instant, the steamed buns are dubious, the "fresh" soy milk isn't—but somehow they manage to keep

the customers coming. Some of the older stores retain the franchise's old logo: a Chinese Colonel Sanders.

Xinianlai
Xǐ'niánlái
喜年来
This is an okay destination for breakfast: they serve Cantonese and Taiwanese snacks 点心 (diǎnxīn; otherwise known as dim sum) for a decent price. The food here will not blow you away, but it's a safe bet when you're hung-over or don't feel like any kind of gastronomical excitement.

Kentucky Fried Chicken
Kěndéjī
肯德基
Known as KFC here in the Middle Kingdom, KFC is more popular than MickeyD's. Maybe it's because they got here early; maybe it's because the Colonel's beard and glasses mark him as a man of learning and cultivation; maybe it's because Chinese tend to prefer chicken and pork to dark meats. KFC has localized its offerings to a greater extent than McDonald's has, and the Macao-style egg-custard tarts are pretty tasty.

Kendeli
Kěndélì
肯德利
A fine introduction to knock-off or "Shanzhai" culture (山寨, shānzhài), Kendeli is a small Chinese fried-chicken franchise that can be found in county seats, small towns, and 3rd tier cities (these cities may have KFC, but Kendeli is cheaper). Not that bad, but every now and then you may get mild food poisoning from it.

Clam Burger
Kěnlàmǔ
肯拉姆
Another "Shanzhai"(山寨, shānzhài) KFC chain based in dire areas of northern China, eating here may even become a weekly event if you are living out in the boonies with no Western food at all. They wanted to call it "Clown Burger" but the tard they hired to do the logos and all the materials wrote "Clam Burger" instead.

McDonald's
Màidāngláo

麦当劳

Chinese McDonald's is just like every other McDonald's in the world, but they speak Chinese. Ronald McDonald is called **麦当劳叔叔** (Màidāngláo Shūshu; "Uncle McDonald") in Chinese, which is creepy but not as creepy as the fact that the waitresses used to be called **麦当劳阿姨** (Màidāngláo Āyí; "Auntie McDonald").

Chinese Burger Home
Zhōngguó Hànbǎo zhī Jiā

中国汉堡之家

This is the "Shanzhai" McDonald's from back before the word "Shanzhai" (**山寨**, shānzhài) meant "knock-off." A lot of them use McDonald's equipment, and if you eat here you'll be getting basically the same food at half the price.

·····Chinese food
Zhōngguó cài
中国菜

Every small town in China has its own local food variants, but the most popular regional cuisines are represented in every city.

Let's go out and eat some…
Zánmen chū qù chī diǎn…ba.

咱们出去吃点 。。。 吧 。

Sichuan food (Szechwan)
Chuān cài

川菜

Sichuan cuisine is known as **麻辣** (málà; numb and spicy). The numb part comes from the abundance of **花椒** (huājiāo), Sichuan peppercorns that tease you by turning up the heat and then numbing your mouth so you can't feel anything. Sichuan cuisine is one of the most popular Chinese regional cuisines, both domestically and internationally. You can find Sichuan restaurants everywhere, but if you want authentic levels of heat you have to ask for it—they think non-Sichuanese folk are chile pussies.

Prickly ash / Sichuan peppercorn
Huājiāo

花椒

Hunan Food
Xiāng cài

湘菜

They say the Hunanese are actually afraid of eating non-spicy-hot food. Perhaps even more than Sichuan food (which occasionally offers dishes that don't bring tears to the eye), this is seriously not for the delicate of tummy. Hunan food has all the flavors: sour, salty, sweet, bitter and always SPICY HOT.

If you are a serious spice freak, ask for extra hot and it will make your head ring, without the feeling of having the inside of your mouth peel off that Thai chiles will give you.

Shanghai food
Shànghǎi cài

上海菜

Renowned for its elegance, Shanghai cuisine is a lesson in subtlety—which is to say that it's oily and bland, but also overpriced. These people put sugar in vinegar.

Northeastern food (Manchurian)
Dōngběi cài

东北菜

As rough and hearty as the Northeasterners themselves, Northeastern food is heavy on potatoes, glass noodles, meat and dumplings. If a thing can be stewed, it's safe to say that the Northeasterners have tried it. Great stuff when you're hungry or when (as is so often the case in Northeastern China) it's thirty degrees below zero out.

Cantonese food
Yuè cài

粤菜

The Cantonese pride themselves on their cuisine, which offers a variety and delicacy not found in other Chinese regional cuisines. They're the ones who brought the world dim sum—and the ones whose cuisine is blamed for starting SARS a few years back. If it walks, slithers, flies, swims or otherwise draws breath, some Cantonese person somewhere has dedicated an amazing amount of thought to eating it.

Xinjiang food
Xīnjiāng cài
新疆菜
Xinjiang Uyghur food is more Central Asian than Chinese—a melange of Silk Road dishes and flavors. There are Xinjiang restaurants everywhere in China with a charcoal kebab grill at the front and at least one or two visibly Uyghur staff in view. If it's a halal (清真, qīngzhēn) Xinjiang restaurant you will get the real deal—steaming fresh rounds of 馕 (náng) flatbread and roast mutton.

Hotpot
Huǒguō
火锅
Hotpot involves a metal pot of simmering broth placed in the middle of the table (usually a concoction of herbs, spices and stock). You order up fresh vegetables, meats, seafood, seaweed, noodles, dumplings and soybean products (豆制品, dòuzhìpǐn) and you dip the food you want to eat into the pot, cook it, then place it the bowl in front of you. There are plenty of dipping sauces to choose from. While the tastiest hotpots are spicy hot, you can order not-spicy hotpots, or you can get the divided pot (half spicy/half non-spicy).

Chongqing hotpot (Chungking hotpot)
Chóngqìng Huǒguō
重庆火锅
There are many different Chongqing hotpot chains and they are all pretty hit and miss, so you may as well just try

your luck. Chongqing hotpot is said to be the spiciest of all hotpots, so if you can't handle chile, this is not for you: some of the places offer mild chicken broth, but that's really defeating the purpose. If you are hell bent on having the authentic Chongqing experience, or are otherwise into pain, ask for extra-spicy (**重辣**, zhònglà). If you have decided to end it all in as spectacular a manner as possible—think spontaneous combustion—ask for "super-very-really-fucking-hot'" (**超级非常真他妈的辣**, chāojí fēicháng zhēn tāmāde là).

Little Sheep Mongolian hotpot (aka, Little Fat Sheep)
Xiǎo Féi Yáng
小肥羊
This hotpot chain is so popular it has crossed the Pacific and can now be found at North American locations, and even Australia! If you're not sure whether to eat the spicy or non-spicy, go for the "Half-Half" hotpot (**鸳鸯锅**; yuānyang guō[2]).

·····Snacks
Xiǎochī
小吃

Listen, save yourself some time and deal with the issue of kitchen hygiene the same way you deal with death and clowns: don't think about it. You might, as some do, opt to eat only at big and expensive restaurants because you're afraid of getting food poisoning; the truth is that the kitchens are just about the same anywhere you go, whether it's a hole-in-the-wall chow mein (**炒面**, chǎomiàn) joint or a hotel's banquet hall. Better to eat at the place you know is dirty than at the place where you can't see the dirt.

The best thing about eating out in China is the vibrant culture and awesome food you'll find at the night markets and street vendors. Although most night markets manifest at fixed

---

2 **鸳鸯锅** (Yuānyang guō) is a much prettier name than "Half-Half," natch. **鸳鸯** (yuānyang) means "Mandarin ducks," a traditional Chinese symbol of marital fidelity. Mandarin duck hotpot has a wavy divide going down the middle, so it looks either like an incomplete "Yin-Yang," or Mandarin ducks locked in a 69 position.

locations, they can potentially exist anywhere. A couple of food vendors with their whole al fresco tricycle-mounted kitchens gathering in one spot is essentially a mini night market. Here are some of the choices at your average night market or street stall snack vendor (these vary with region):

Let's get some snacks!
Wǒmen chī ba!

们吃吧！

Mutton kebabs
Yángròu chuànr

羊肉串儿

This is considered by most Western people who like to drink as the ultimate drunk food, usually operated by Uygur or Hui (ethnically Chinese Muslims), often strategically located near bars and clubs. "Mutton" is probably an optimistic description of what's being sold here, but it's tasty all the same.

Street BBQ
Shāokǎo

烧烤

Although Xinjiang kebabs are the most well known type of street snack among the Westerners fresh off the boat, the Chinese really dig their general BBQ. You can choose almost any vegetable available to be char grilled (the safer option if you are worried about the meat that's been sitting in the Styrofoam box all night in the middle of summer), or chicken wings, hearts, squid, fish, etc., for meat eaters. Get a bunch of friends, grab a table with the little plastic chairs, order a shitload of beer, maybe even get a keg if it's a large night market. If your are flying solo, just wait till some curious locals start calling out "Hello!" then refer to "Angry Chinese" and call them stupid. They'll be shocked at first, then laugh, then invite you over to join in on the BBQ madness. You will get extremely drunk.

Dapaidang
Dàpáidàng

大排档

This is basically street stir fry, just as popular as the BBQ above, similar setting, same tips for drinking with locals.

Spicy flash-boiled things
Málàtáng

麻辣烫

Málàtáng is from Chongqing (formerly part of Sichuan Province). You pick out the fresh ingredients you want from the fridge—bamboo shoots, meat balls, various tofu iterations, greens, shrooms, seaweed (yeah, you get the idea)—putting them in a basket as you go. Pay first, then they put all your shit into a steel basket and submerge it in the bubbling spicy soup in the 40-gallon drum. When it's cooked they add the chile oil, and the fried chile flakes (optional), your choice of garlic, cilantro and spring onion. Málàtáng can be found everywhere in China, but the most authentic is made by Chongqingers. If you can speak Chinese, just talk to the boss and listen for the lilting Sichuan accent (they sound like Chinese leprechauns). Don't think too hard about the sanitation.

Shengjian (pan-fried pork buns)
Shēngjiān

生煎

Shengjian is a Yangtze River delta street food. They make the little pork buns, then put them in a huge shallow pan of bubbling oil (enough to fry only the bottom of the bun). Cover the pan with a bamboo lid and then violently rotate the pan every minute. Don't be surprised if you have to queue up for these. Be careful of the hot juices sealed inside the buns—eating them is harder than it looks, but you'll figure it out after the first few times you burn your lips.

•••••Weird shit
Yěwèi

野味

In Beijing you'll see the starfish and scorpion kebabs at the "official" food street in Wangfujing. If you really want bragging rights back home, skip the touristy gimmicks (locals don't even eat them) and eat authentic weird shit—some of it actually tastes good! When your Chinese friends ask you what you feel like for dinner, tell 'em you want to try their local "peasant food" (土菜, tǔcài). This could turn out to be the best Chinese food you've ever had—if not the best, then at least the most authentic. Amongst the fairly normal looking food, you'll be served up stuff more suited to the "Temple of Doom" banquet. This is weird shit in real context.

Now there's weird and there's weird (by non-Chinese standards). You gotta understand that for the Chinese, nothing is weird, so if you ask 'em if you're about to eat weird local specialties (**特别风味**, tèbié fēngwèi; literally, "unusual local flavors"), they'll honestly say no.

Ducks heads (spicy)
Yātóu
鸭头

Spicy rabbit heads
Málà tùzi tóu
麻辣兔子头

Spicy tripe (preserved duck's blood and eel stew)
Máoxuěwàng
毛血旺

Silk worm chrysalis
Cányǒng
蚕蛹

Fried cicadas
Jīnchán
金蝉
Literally, "gold cicadas."

Little fried scorpion
Yóuzhà xiēzi
油炸蝎子
These taste like french fries.

Sparrows
Máquè
麻雀

Duck tongue
Yāshé
鸭舌

"Three Treasures"
Jíxiáng sānbǎo
吉祥三宝
The three treasures in question: bull penis, goat testicles and chicken kidney.

Fish air bladder (in hotpot)
Yúbiào
鱼鳔

••••• Yuck!
Nánchī!
难吃！

There's so much good food here in China, but there is also an abundance of shite. Either it's too exotic for your taste experience, or it's just poorly made.

On your first visit, you'll either love the food or decide that it doesn't agree with you. Either way, it takes experience to tell the difference between something that is cooked well and something you wouldn't even inflict upon your pet alligator. Not only will you come across stuff that tastes bad, you'll experience tasty food that will leave you with an ass that thinks it's a sprinkler. So here are a couple of phrases that will help your gracious hosts understand that they shouldn't order the pig intestines for you next time.

This tastes weird.
Chīqǐái **guàiguài de**.
吃起来**怪怪的** 。

This tastes bad.
Bù hǎochī.
不好吃 。

Too disgusting.
Tài ěxīn.
太恶心 。

This is sooo bad!
Tài nánchī!
太难吃 ！

This is as bad as it can get.
Nánchī zhìjí.
难吃至极 。

Fucking gross!
Zhēn tāmāde nán chī!
真他妈的难吃 ！

I can't eat this shit!
Wǒ chī bù xià qù!
我吃不下去 ！

This restaurant fucking sucks!
Zhège **fàndiàn** tài tāmāde chàjìn le!
这个**饭店**太他妈的差劲了 ！

This is worse than eating feces.
Bǐ shǐ hái nán chī.
比屎还难吃 。

This doesn't even compare with dog shit.
Lián **gǒush**ǐ dōu bù rú.
连**狗屎**都不如 。
Dog shit would be better.

So bad I can't swallow.
Nán yǐ xiàyàn.
难以下咽 。

Disgusting in so many messy ways.
Nánchī de yītāhútu.
难吃的一塌糊涂 。

Jail food beats this shit hands down!
Zhège cài bǐ **láofàn** hái nán chī!
这个菜比**牢饭**还难吃！

This gave me food poisoning.
Zhège fàn ràng wǒ **shíwù zhòngdú** le.
这个饭让我**食物中毒**了。

Let's go.
Zǒu ba.
走吧。

Let's skip out on the check.
Bàwángcān.
霸王餐。
Literally, "King's Meal" (i.e., you avoid paying).

Everything that is alive is a potential meal. A friend of mine was bragging about how he got hold of an anteater (illegal to possess, let alone eat) and proceeded to show me great respect by asking me to join him in enjoying this delicacy. Our relationship is at the level where I could safely turn down the offer and then proceed to express my disapproval of his intended feast. When I asked why he (Chinese people) would want to eat such exotic, not to mention protected, creatures, his reply was lightning fast: "It's simple—if it is alive, if it breathes, I have the uncontrollable desire to know what it tastes like. It would be unbearable to be lying on my deathbed knowing that in my life I'd passed up the opportunity to eat something I'd not yet tried."

Dirty French: Everyday Slang from "What's Up?" to "F*%# Off!"
ADRIEN CLAUTRIER & HENRY ROWE, **$10.00**

With this book, you can use sweet words to entice a local beauty into a walk along the Seine, and less-than-philosophical rebuffs for those zealous, espresso-fueled cafe "poets." There are enough insults and swear words to offend every person in France without even speaking to them in English.

Dirty German: Everyday Slang from "What's Up?" to "F*%# Off!"
DANIEL CHAFFEY, **$10.00**

Dirty German provides plenty of insults and swear words to piss off every person in Germany—without even mentioning that the Japanese make better cars —as well as explicit sex terms that'll even embarrass the women of Hamburg's infamous red light district.

Dirty Italian: Everyday Slang from "What's Up?" to "F*%# Off!"
GABRIELLE EUVINO, **$10.00**

This useful guide contains phrases for every situation, including insults to hurl at the refs during *fútbol* games. Readers learn sweet words to entice a local beauty into a romantic gondola ride, not-so-sweet remarks to ward off any overzealous Venetians, and more.

Dirty Japanese: Everyday Slang from "What's Up?" to "F*%# Off!"
MATT FARGO, **$10.00**

Even in traditionally minded Japan, slang from its edgy pop culture constantly enter into common usage. This book fills in the gap between how people really talk in Japan and what Japanese language students are taught.

Dirty Korean: Everyday Slang from "What's Up?" to "F*%# Off!"
HAEWON BAEK, **$10.00**

This book presents cool things to say for all casual situations — shopping, parties, nightclubs, sporting events, and even romance and sex. There's even sex terminology graphic enough to embarrass even the most jaded hostess at a massage parlor.

Dirty Russian: Everyday Slang from "What's Up?" to "F*%# Off!"
ERIN COYNE & IGOR FISUN, **$10.00**

An invaluable guide for off-the-beaten-path travelers going to Russia, *Dirty Russian* is packed with enough insults and swear words to offend every person in Russia without even mentioning that they lost the Cold War.

Dirty Spanish: Everyday Slang from "What's Up?" to "F*%# Off!"
JUAN CABALLERO & NICK DENTON-BROWN, **$10.00**

This handbook features slang for both Spain and Latin America. It includes a section on native banter that will help readers make friends over a pitcher of sangría and convince the local taco maker that it's OK to spice things up with a few fresh habaneros.

To order these books call 800-377-2542 or 510-601-8301, fax 510-601-8307, e-mail ulysses@ulyssespress.com, or write to Ulysses Press, P.O. Box 3440, Berkeley, CA 94703. All retail orders are shipped free of charge. California residents must include sales tax. Allow two to three weeks for delivery.

•••••About the Authors

Matt Coleman is a Univeristy of Queensland Chinese Language graduate who has spent six years in China—long enough to know that understanding foul language is a very important and essential skill that must be used wisely. He likes China, spicy food, and Scotch single malt whiskeys. He wants to eat home-cooked meals in every country he possibly can.

Edmund Backhouse is the nom de guerre of a Beijing-based writer and translator. Despite his potty mouth and his choice of namesake, he leads a relatively virtuous life.